FOUL DEEDS & SUSPICIOUS DEATHS
IN SHREWSBURY
AND AROUND SHROPSHIRE

TRUE CRIME FROM WHARNCLIFFE

Foul Deeds and Suspicious Deaths Series

Barking, Dagenham & Chadwell Heath
Barnsley
Bath
Bedford
Birmingham
More Foul Deeds Birmingham
Black Country
Blackburn and Hyndburn
Bolton
Bradford
Brighton
Bristol
Cambridge
Carlisle
Chesterfield
Cumbria
More Foul Deeds Chesterfield
Colchester
Coventry
Croydon
Derby
Durham
Ealing
Fens
Folkstone and Dover
Grimsby
Guernsey
Guildford
Halifax
Hampstead, Holborn and St Pancras

Huddersfield
Hull
Jersey
Leeds
Leicester
Lewisham and Deptford
Liverpool
London's East End
London's West End
Manchester
Mansfield
More Foul Deeds Wakefield
Newcastle
Newport
Norfolk
Northampton
Nottingham
Oxfordshire
Pontefract and Castleford
Portsmouth
Rotherham
Scunthorpe
Southend-on-Sea
Southport
Staffordshire and the Potteries
Stratford and South Warwickshire
Tees
Warwickshire
Wigan
York

OTHER TRUE CRIME BOOKS FROM WHARNCLIFFE

A-Z of London Murders
A-Z of Yorkshire Murders
Black Barnsley
Brighton Crime and Vice 1800-2000
Durham Executions
Essex Murders
Executions & Hangings in Newcastle
    and Morpeth
Norfolk Mayhem and Murder

Norwich Murders
Strangeways Hanged
Unsolved Murders in Victorian &
    Edwardian London
Unsolved Norfolk Murders
Unsolved Yorkshire Murders
Warwickshire's Murderous Women
Yorkshire Hangmen
Yorkshire's Murderous Women

Please contact us via any of the methods below for more information
or a catalogue
WHARNCLIFFE BOOKS
47 Church Street, Barnsley, South Yorkshire, S70 2AS
Tel: 01226 734555 • 734222 • Fax: 01226 734438
email: enquiries@pen-and-sword.co.uk
website: www.wharncliffebooks.co.uk

Foul Deeds & Suspicious Deaths In

SHREWSBURY

And Around

SHROPSHIRE

David J Cox

Wharncliffe Books

First Published in Great Britain in 2008 by
Wharncliffe Books
an imprint of
Pen and Sword Books Limited,
47 Church Street, Barnsley,
South Yorkshire. S70 2AS

Copyright © David J Cox, 2008

ISBN: 978 1 845630 706

A CIP catalogue record of this book is available from the
British Library

Typeset in Plantin and Benguiat by
Pen and Sword Books Ltd

Printed in the United Kingdom by
CPI Antony Rowe

Pen & Sword Books Ltd incorporates the imprints of
Pen & Sword Aviation, Pen & Sword Maritime,
Pen & Sword Military, Wharncliffe Local History, Pen & Sword Select,
Pen & Sword Military Classics, Leo Cooper, Remember When, Seaforth Publishing
and Frontline Publishing

For a complete list of Pen & Sword titles please contact:
PEN & SWORD BOOKS LIMITED
47 Church Street, Barnsley, South Yorkshire, S70 2AS, England.
E-mail: enquiries@pen-and-sword.co.uk
Website: www.pen-and-sword.co.uk

Contents

Acknowledgements

I would like to acknowledge the help and assistance given to me by the staff of the numerous archives, libraries and record offices visited during the course of my research. Special thanks must go to Mary McKenzie (County Archivist) and Armand De Filippo (Principal Librarian) together with all their colleagues at the Shropshire Archives and Record Centre, who provided unfailingly courteous help and advice, Birmingham Central Reference Library, Chester Archives, Keele University Library, The National Archives, Kew, University of Birmingham Library, The Queen's Dragoon Guards Regimental Museum, Cardiff, and the Archives Office of Tasmania.

The majority of photographic images in the book have been taken by the author. Due permission has been sought and sources credited for those other illustrations that remain in copyright. Many thanks are given to Shropshire Archives and Record Centre for their permission to reproduce images of several items in their care.

A lawyer and his client, 1572.
Author's collection

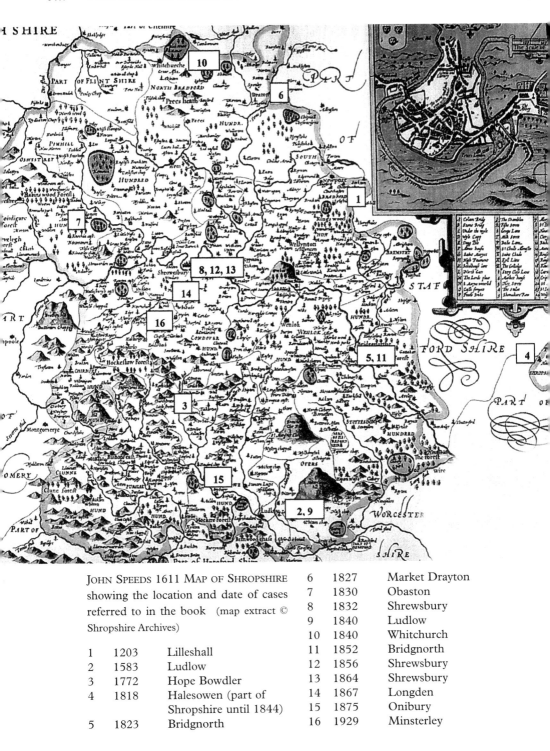

JOHN SPEEDS 1611 MAP OF SHROPSHIRE
showing the location and date of cases
referred to in the book (map extract ©
Shropshire Archives)

6	1827	Market Drayton
7	1830	Obaston
8	1832	Shrewsbury
9	1840	Ludlow
10	1840	Whitchurch
11	1852	Bridgnorth
12	1856	Shrewsbury
13	1864	Shrewsbury
14	1867	Longden
15	1875	Onibury
16	1929	Minsterley

1	1203	Lilleshall
2	1583	Ludlow
3	1772	Hope Bowdler
4	1818	Halesowen (part of Shropshire until 1844)
5	1823	Bridgnorth

Introduction

Crime has always exerted a fascination over us and it continues so to do: witness the often lurid headlines to be found in almost every daily newspaper or the plethora of detective stories featured in radio or television programmes, both factual and fictional – *Poirot, CSI, Crimewatch, Inspector Morse* etc – all of which we avidly devour.

This book contains a wide variety of suspicious deaths and foul deeds that have a Shrewsbury or Shropshire connection over an 800-year period from the early Middle Ages through to the early decades of the twentieth century. The object of this publication is not merely to recite dramatic cases of murder – to do so would involve little more than a simple narrative regurgitation of contemporary newspaper reports of trials and would rapidly become repetitive. Instead, whilst hopefully engaging readers' attention with sixteen cases that cover many types of crime over an extensive chronological period, I have sought to relate each of the cases to wider developments in the history of criminal detection, justice and punishment in England.

The background and known facts of each case have therefore been conscientiously and meticulously researched using a wide variety of both primary and secondary sources including assize records, calendars of prisoners, court records, census returns, newspaper reports etc., in order to provide a wide cross-section of foul deeds and suspicious deaths from around Shrewsbury and Shropshire. Cases detailed in the book include arson, bigamy, fraud, imposture, infanticide, and several murders, together with often reprehensible and occasionally atrocious behaviour by the forces of justice and law and order.

Several of the cases illustrate a particular aspect of crime, detection or punishment, such as the absence of what we would now recognize as a police force; the difficulty of proving the identity of a murderer due to the limitations of forensic science; the different ways in which men and women were treated before the law; and the often brutal forms of punishment that were meted out to convicted offenders, especially in the Middle Ages and the early-modern period of English history.

Within its pages can be found all the elements of criminality that so intrigue us: murder, violence, bad behaviour, detection, punishment, sometimes unintentional humour, and perhaps even occasional sneaking admiration for an audacious rogue.

Unfortunately no national crime statistics were kept before 1805, so it is impossible to accurately compare crime figures from the past with those that are reported today. However, human nature has changed little over time, and, as the following pages will show, crime of all kinds was far from absent in Shrewsbury and around Shropshire in the preceding centuries. Each generation seems inclined to hark back to a mythical 'golden age', and this is certainly the case when discussing crime. Consider the following two statements:

Highway robbery and burglary were common. It was not safe to go out after dark.

It was not safe to go out at night owing to the profusion of housebreakers, highwaymen, and footpads – and especially because of the savage barbarity of the two latter, who commit the most wanton cruelties.

Either of these statements could have appeared in newspaper columns within the past few weeks (with just a few minor idiomatic alterations), illustrating a perceived breakdown of law and order in contemporary society. In fact, the first was written in the 1880s about the 1840s by a Victorian diarist and poacher, James Hawker, whilst the second was penned in October 1751 by Westminster magistrate and famous novelist Henry Fielding, indicating that there has always been a strong societal worry about the amount of crime present in each generation.

Whilst Britain has been fortunate in recent years in having developed a reasonably robust and fair legislature and judiciary, together with largely democratically accountable police forces (although the extent of this accountability has been recently increasingly questioned), this has not always been the case. This book illustrates that many of the constituents forming the bedrock of our present criminal justice system, including the right to defend oneself before a jury; the right to a fair trial; the right to appeal after judgement; the existence of an efficient and unbiased police force; the need for prosecutors to prove a defendant's guilt rather than a defendant prove his/her innocence; and the reliance on judges and juries to be apolitical and impartial, are in fact all relatively modern constructs. Many of our predecessors (especially if poor) could not depend on most of these rights. In certain ways the criminal justice system has changed almost beyond recognition in the past 800 years, and this is primarily reflected in the methods of punishment to which an offender was sentenced – those detailed in this book include having one's eyes gouged out, one's ear nailed to a board, death (often slow and painful) by hanging, or being forcibly transported to a new country, thousands of miles away from one's home, family and friends.

I have endeavoured to give readers a flavour of some of the foul deeds and suspicious deaths that have occurred in Shrewsbury and throughout Shropshire during the past eight centuries, and have chosen a wide cross-section of cases that hopefully will engage people's interest. I have also tried to show the human aspect of all the cases; the people detailed within the book all existed and either suffered their occasionally awful fate or carried out foul deeds in reality; these events actually happened and therefore should not be seen merely as stories by which to frighten or entertain ourselves. Some of the offences and their aftermath, as illustrated in the book, could be extremely brutal and inhumane, both in terms of offence and punishment. Although many of the cases do possess sensational aspects (and were reported in such a manner), I have tried to ensure that they are not related in an unduly voyeuristic or salacious manner. Similarly, in order to avoid distress, discomfort or offence to any living relatives or friends of those involved as either victims or perpetrators, no case featured is more recent than the early twentieth century.

It is to be hoped that readers enjoy learning about the cases detailed in the following pages and that they are also stimulated to find out more about England's fascinating criminal justice history. A brief *Further Reading* section is therefore provided at the end of the book in order to point any readers that may be thus inspired in the necessary direction.

Finally, although the most meticulous care has been taken to ensure the accuracy of facts and events of each case detailed within the following pages, it must be appreciated that the book deals with records of cases that occurred a considerable time ago, with several of the primary documentary sources surviving somewhat patchily over a period of many centuries. As a consequence, there are occasions in which different sources give different versions of events, with often conflicting details or outcomes; indeed in one or two of the cases the outcome remains unknown. Any such errors or omissions that may have arisen as a result are therefore apologized for in advance.

A brief note on the English legal system

Several aspects of the English trial-based legal system, although being subject to several important changes throughout the centuries (as will become apparent through reading this book), have in essence remained remarkably similar in their constitution from at least the thirteenth century. During the majority of the period covered by this book, criminal cases were first brought before a justice of the peace or magistrate (the terms are interchangeable, although current court usage favours the term magistrate) at either Petty Sessions (which could occur as and when the need arose and were usually held at a local community venue such as a public house or, from the latter half of the nineteenth century, in a purpose-built magistrates' court) or, for more serious cases, Quarter Sessions, which, as their name implies, were held every quarter (March, June, September and December), usually in the larger towns of a county.

These were presided over by county magistrates and were heard before a jury. In cases where the magistrates felt that they were unqualified to deal with the complicated or extremely serious nature of the crime, defendants could be held in gaol for a considerable period to await trial at the Assizes, which were presided over by royally or (more latterly) state-appointed judges, and which normally took place twice a year, usually in the county town – in this case, Shrewsbury – at Lent (March/April) and Trinity or Summer (July/August). A third Assize court, known as the

Winter Assizes could also be held (usually sometime between October and December) if warranted by the number of cases waiting to be tried in any particular year. The system of Petty Sessions, Quarter Sessions and Assizes was completely swept away by the passing of the Courts Act of 1971, which replaced the old system with Magistrates' Courts (which deal with petty offences) and the Crown Court (which hears more serious criminal cases).

Pre-decimal currency system
Throughout this book the pre-decimal system of currency is used. Prior to decimalization in 1971, the British currency system was based on the ancient system of LSD or £ (pound) s. (shillings) and d. (pence). £1 was made up of 240 pennies (because a pound of silver was used in Anglo-Saxon times to make that number of silver pennies), twelve of which made a shilling. The penny itself was subdivided into farthings (four of which made a penny) or halfpennies (two of which made a penny). A guinea was worth £1 and one shilling (i.e. twenty-one shillings). It is extremely difficult to accurately equate monetary values from historical periods to those of the present-day, due to the fluctuating costs of basic goods and foods, but a rough multiplication of between 100 and 125 should be made to late-eighteenth and early-nineteenth-century figures in order to compare them with present-day values, whilst late-nineteenth-century figures should be multiplied by around 50 to arrive at a general modern-day comparison.

Stocks and whipping post, Norton, Shropshire. The Author

Chapter 1

'Almost to the extreme limit of legal memory'
Murder in Lilleshall
1203

This chapter illustrates how the early medieval justice system functioned, and how the justice meted out could be swift and horrifically brutal. The case is also interesting in that it serves to show how medieval monarchs (in this instance King John), although in many ways extremely powerful, could also remain subservient to the laws of the Church.

The English legal system has its origins in the system of criminal justice created by Anglo-Saxon kings such as Ethelbert (c.552-616) and Alfred the Great (849-99), who both developed and issued a system of law-codes which remained in use throughout the Anglo-Saxon period. Following the Norman Conquest much of this systematic law-code remained in use, including the use of 'hue and cry', whereby every member of a parish was legally required to pursue and capture suspected criminals. Failure to do so could involve legal action in the form of levying fines.

King Henry II – creator of the Royal Justices in 1166. Author's collection

However, the Norman kings also introduced several new ideas in the field of criminal justice. One of the most notable of these was the decision in 1166 of King Henry II (1133-89) to instigate a system by which royally appointed Justices would visit each of the shires or counties hearing 'pleas of the Crown' (cases between the king's subjects) on a regular basis on behalf of the king. The king had previously dispensed justice throughout the country personally, but this was problematic as many of the Norman kings were peripatetic, spending large amounts of their time in their French dominions, and therefore there was no guarantee when cases would be heard. For example King John was in France (where he also held land) from May 1201 until December 1203, and would have been unable to hear any cases in person. Therefore it was decreed that twelve free men from each hundred (a division of a county) would present cases that had occurred in each county to these visiting Royal Justices who would hear the evidence in a court, deliberate and then pass sentence on the suspects.

These perambulations of the Royal Justices became known as Eyres (from the Latin *errāre* – to wander) and the Justices in Eyre quickly became the most visible indication of the king's power and presence with regard to the legal and judicial affairs of the shires. The courts could sit for a considerable time and hear a great many cases – for example, the Shropshire Eyre of 1256 sat at Shrewsbury from Friday, 14 January to Wednesday, 16 February, hearing almost 500 civil cases and over 400 criminal cases. This system gradually evolved until by the middle of the thirteenth century it became the more recognizable system of Assizes (which lasted until the twentieth century), in which senior royally appointed judges would ride out into the counties at least twice a year in order to hear serious criminal cases.

A record of these Eyres (known as Eyre Rolls as they were originally written down on parchment rolls) was kept by clerks from the first, and we are lucky that many of them have survived the intervening centuries (some seventy exist from the time of King John alone), providing us with a fascinating glimpse into the ways in which early medieval justice functioned. These surviving documents have been memorably described by the historian F W

Maitland as being 'almost to the extreme limit of legal memory'. Originally written in clerical Latin, many of the documents have been subsequently translated into English and published for the use of historians.

One of the earliest such Eyre Rolls to have survived is the Shropshire Eyre Roll of 1203. This details pleas of the Crown heard from the various hundreds of Shropshire which were placed before the four royal justices: William de Cantilupe, Simon of Pattishall, Henry of Northampton and Richard of Seetling (surnames were not commonly used until the latter part of the thirteenth century). On Wednesday, 1 October 1203 the court heard details of a murder and robbery that had occurred earlier in the year at Lilleshall.

Lilleshall is recorded in *Domesday Book* as a small settlement, and remained so throughout the Middle Ages (despite nearby Lilleshall Abbey being founded in the mid-twelfth century):

> *The church* [St Alkmund] *held and holds Lilleshall. There are ten hides* [an amount of land that would support a household]. *In demesne* [land whose produce is devoted to the lord of the manor rather than his tenants] *are two ploughs* [measure of arable capacity of the land]; *and ten villans* [peasants] *and five bordars* [lesser peasants] *and three French* [immigrant peasants, not necessarily from France] *sergeants* [tenants who performed a specific service such as a forester] *with eight ploughs among them all, and there might be nine ploughs more. There are four oxmen, and a mill, but it renders nothing. There is a league of woodland. In the reign of Edward* [i.e. before the Norman Conquest] *it was worth £6, now £4. Godebold the priest holds it.*

Four men (Elias, Geoffrey and Robert of Lilleshall, and Peter of Hopton) and four women (Eva, Aldith and Mabel of Lilleshall, and Alice Crithecreche) were charged with the murder of an unnamed woman who was slain at Lilleshall. There would very likely have been a coroner's inquest into this death prior to the trial (the office of Coroner dates back to the late twelfth century, and four coroners were appointed for each county), but unfortunately the records do not survive in regard to this case.

One of the suspects, Elias of Lilleshall, managed to escape the

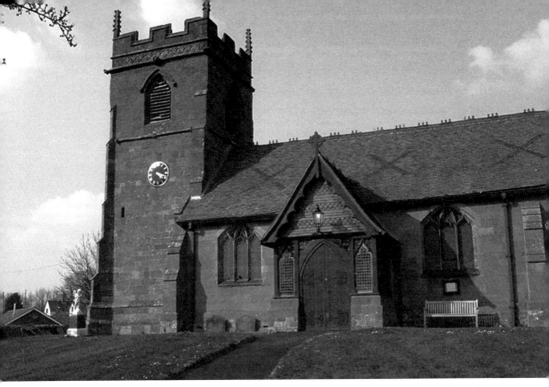

St Michael and All Angels Church, Lilleshall. Parts of the present church would have been familiar to Elias of Lilleshall as he fled to the building in search of sanctuary. Some of the earliest extant masonry belongs to the southern doorway in the nave and it is not inconceivable that Elias passed through it during his sojourn there. The Author

clutches of the Crown by fleeing to the nearby church of St Michael and All Angels in Lilleshall, where he confessed to the murder to the no doubt shocked priest, and immediately claimed the right of sanctuary.

The right of sanctuary was an ancient privilege afforded by the Church, as a result of which any man suspected of a serious crime (with the exceptions of sacrilege or high treason) could claim shelter and immunity from prosecution if he succeeded in getting to a church before he was caught as a result of the raised 'hue and cry'. Once in the church the suspected person was deemed to be 'in mercy'; he had to wear clerical garb and could remain in the safety of the church for a period of forty days. If, whilst he was in the care of the Church, he chose to confess his sins he would not be tried but instead would be allowed to 'abjure the realm'. This was a form of self-imposed exile, by which the man would be escorted to a major seaport assigned by the king's Coroner (usually the one nearest the place of sanctuary – in this case it could well have been either Chester or Bristol) and put onto the next foreign-bound ship. If the man subsequently returned to the shores of England or Wales he risked being immediately executed without trial.

The survival of the right of sanctuary clearly depended upon the balance of power between the secular reigning monarch and the spiritual authority of the Church. It is interesting to note that the right of sanctuary, although being partially abolished in 1493, was not finally ended until the early seventeenth century during the reign of King James I. Although various individuals (with or without the explicit sanction of the monarch) undoubtedly did breach the sanctity of sanctuary, many kings were loathe to risk their spiritual souls (and perhaps their temporal authority) by openly challenging the status quo. A surviving register of writs issued by King Edward II (a monarch who undoubtedly had his own share of problems with regard to authority) and dated to 1318-20 illustrates that at least in one case the monarch was unwilling to challenge the Church's supremacy in this matter:

FOR THE RETURN TO A CHURCH OF ONE DRAGGED THEREFROM

From King Edward II to his Justice assigned to deliver the gaol at T–: The venerable father R–, bishop of Carlisle, informed us by his letters patent that, whereas A–, lately taken and detained in our prison [...] for a crime of theft attested against him, had escaped from the said prison and fled to the sanctuary of the said church, certain malefactors, unmindful of their salvation, going to the said church, violently dragged the said prisoner from the aforementioned church and carried him off to Carlisle and delivered him to our Sheriff of the aforesaid county to be constrained in prison, in which he is still detained to the painful prejudice of ecclesiastical liberty. As we are unwilling that ecclesiastical liberty should in any way be infringed by us or by our ministers, we command you that, if you establish the facts to be as alleged, you shall cause the said A– to the same place from which he was dragged out, as it is said, to remain there in the same condition as at the time of the aforesaid dragging forth, according to ecclesiastical liberty.

Elias of Lilleshall could perhaps consider himself to be a very fortunate individual in that King John, his ministers or any relatives of the deceased woman did not challenge the right of sanctuary in this case. It is specifically mentioned that Elias possessed no chattels (goods) and was therefore not to be considered a man of substance or quality, who would have been able to offer to make amends for his crime to relatives of the victim by means of financial recompense in the form of 'blood-money'.

However, another of the suspects in the case did not fare so well. Alice Crithecreche was one of the four women implicated in the murder. The records tell us that immediately after the murder, Alice fled into the neighbouring county of Stafford with some of the stolen goods. She may have thought that she was safe after she had managed to escape to Staffordshire, as the legal jurisdiction of the Sheriff (the king's local law-enforcement official) only stretched as far as the individual county, and the hue and cry was normally only enforced at a parochial level.

However, if Alice did presuppose this, she was sadly mistaken in this instance, as the Sheriff of Shropshire from 1198-1204 was Geoffrey FitzPeter, the 1st earl of Essex, who was not only also the Sheriff of Staffordshire from 1201-04, but was also the Chief Justiciar of England. As such he was the most senior legal officer in the country and presided over courts throughout England in the absence of the king. A hue and cry therefore ensued, and Alice was hastily followed and seized, being brought back into Shropshire by the king's officials, whereby she immediately told of an alleged dastardly plot in which she was the unwitting participant. She stated that on the night of the murder she was near the house of the victim and looked through a chink in the door upon hearing a tumult. She saw four men who immediately grabbed hold of her and threatened to kill her unless she promised to conceal them. For this service she stated that she was given half the *pelf* (dishonestly acquired goods) that the men had taken from their victim.

It seems that Alice thought this story up in a hurry, because by the time she appeared before the Justice she denied all, presumably choosing to throw herself upon the mercy of the court. Once again she was unfortunate. The Eyre Roll records that whilst the remaining suspects were found not guilty (but were however put under pledges – similar to being bound over to be of good behaviour), Alice was found guilty of both murder and attempting to pervert the course of justice. As a convicted murderer, she would normally have faced the death penalty but her sentence was instead reduced to that of *sed per dipensacionem eruantur ei oculi* – having her eyes gouged out. The sentence may have been 'mitigated' in response to her gender; female murderers were (and remain) much rarer than their male counterparts.

The extreme physical nature of Alice's horrendous punishment, though somewhat unusual, was not that rare in medieval England, although the particular barbarity of gouging out of eyes was more often used for those who had flouted the very strict forestry or game laws; a twelfth-century chronicler, Henry of Huntingdon, stated that 'whoever shall kill a stag, a wild boar, or even a hare, shall have his eyes gouged out'. Sentences for convicted murderers such as Alice were usually capital in nature and often involved a considerable amount of deliberately inflicted severe incidental pain. As Professor Trishia Olson has pointed out in a recent article on medieval punishment, *The medieval Blood Sanction and the Divine Benificence of Pain 1100-1450*:

> *Grisly images of an executioner dismembering a condemned's limbs from his torso, smashing his chest cavity, gouging his eyes, or piercing his body with hot pokers are the common subject of scaffold art in the high Middle Ages. Such images attest to the critical role of pain in medieval capital punishment.*

Such barbaric acts were clearly designed to act as a kind of preventative jurisprudence; the severity and deliberate suffering inflicted upon those found guilty was undoubtedly meant to serve as a dire warning of the consequences of straying from the straight and narrow. To further reinforce the message the punishment would have been carried out in public and crowds encouraged to witness the scene. There was also perhaps a 'redemptive' element in the infliction of such suffering; the victim could be seen to undergo a similar experience of brutality to that of Christ's suffering on the cross, which would ultimately lead them to spiritual salvation. Whatever the underlying motives for the punishment, such mutilation must have had a devastating effect on Alice even supposing that she survived the terrible shock and pain of the sentence being carried out. Unfortunately no documents survive to tell us of her subsequent fate.

Chapter 2

'Be humble and obedient to your masters'

Forgery in Ludlow

1583

This chapter shows that the often brutal and corporal punishment of the high Middle Ages continued through to the early-modern period. It also illustrates that several influential Elizabethans were concerned about the quality of the judicial system in Shropshire and the Welsh Marches, and that this concern reached right to the top of the political tree.

Sir Henry Sidney (1529-86) was the head of one of the most important and powerful aristocratic families in England during the reign of Queen Elizabeth I. As the son of a courtier, he had spent much of his youth in the company of the only legitimate son of King Henry VIII, the short-lived Edward VI, and was knighted by his childhood friend in 1550. It was reputed that the sickly young man had died in his arms in 1553, and despite the troubles of Queen Mary's reign, Henry continued to prosper, and remained on good terms with Edward's half-sister, who was to become Queen Elizabeth I in 1558. He was appointed Lord Deputy of Ireland in 1565, resigned the post in 1571 and was re-appointed from 1575-78.

Although the Sidney family seat was at Penshurst in Kent, Sir Henry had several connections with Shropshire, including becoming Lord President of the Council of the Marches in 1559 (a post that he retained until his death in Ludlow on 5 May 1589). The Council of the Marches administered the whole of Wales and the five English counties that bordered the principality (including Shropshire), and its duties included the control of local justice; as a contemporary State Paper of 1575 states, 'the Councell in the

Sir Henry Sidney in his role as Lord Deputy of Ireland. Author's collection

marches of Wales was established for the punishment of felonies
and murthers *(murders)*, with the suppression of ryottes *(riots)*,
rowtes *(routs)* and other misdemeynors *(misdemeanours)*'.   The
headquarters of the Council was Ludlow Castle, and as President
of the Council, Sir Henry was responsible for much of the
sixteenth-century rebuilding of the castle (then a royal property),
including the beautiful Judges' Lodgings, which were completed in
1581, and which contain a magnificently carved Sidney coat of
arms with his motto *Hominibus Ingratis Loqvimini Lapides* – 'To
Ungrateful Men We Stones Do Speak'. The post was accompanied
with a fair degree of ceremony, as the following account of the
procession of Sir Henry in Shrewsbury on St George's Day, 1581

shows:

> *Sir Henry Sidney kept St George's Day feast most honourably, coming the said day from the Council House in his knightly robes most valiantly with his gentleman before him and his knights following him in brave order and after them the bailiffs and aldermen in their scarlet gowns with the companies of all occupations in the said town in their best liveries.*

Sir Henry was also father to the rather more famous Sir Philip Sidney (1554-86), who apart from being a successful soldier and international diplomat, was a talented poet who led a literary circle including Edmund Spenser and Fulke Greville. After his short life, his posthumous reputation as a poet of considerable merit grew throughout the succeeding centuries. Sir Philip spent some of his early schooldays at Shrewsbury School (established in 1552), and later married Frances, the daughter of Sir Francis Walsingham (c. 1532-1590), spymaster to Queen Elizabeth.

Sir Henry, in his position as Lord President of the Council of the Marches, had a considerable amount of dealings with the administration of justice in Shropshire and the other border

Ludlow Castle, with the Great Tower (centre-left) and the Judges' Lodgings (centre-right), with Sir Henry Sidney's impressive coat of arms above the entrance doorway. The Author

counties. A letter sent to him from Queen Elizabeth I on 11 June 1567 suggests that neither he nor the monarch were too impressed by the standard of the justices of the peace of the area:

> *We perceive by your letters and have thought it always to be true, that the insufficiency of our justices, both of our benches* (local courts) *and of our Common Pleas* (which dealt primarily with civil rather than criminal cases), *with others in our Exchequer* (responsible for Royal revenue), *is a special hindrance to our service, and a lack to the due administration of justice, wherefore we do like well to have them charged and some sent from hence to hold their places.*

Queen Elizabeth was therefore directing Sir Henry to replace some of the less efficient justices with personally approved individuals. However, in the same letter Elizabeth also goes on to reprimand Sir Henry himself, suggesting that he had overstepped the mark with regard to his position:

> *In some other [of] your letters also we find that which we cannot like, that so small regard should be had of us, as you cannot content yourself, if we should dispense the office which you hold to be President of our Council in Wales, upon any other person, but that you would also thereupon be ready to leave that which you have [...] we allow not of such precise terms as you claim.*

In other words, Sir Henry should not dare question the authority of the queen to appoint whom she wanted in any post, and he should not presume to set terms for his continued employment in the service of the monarch.

During Sir Henry's time as Lord President of the Council of the Marches, a case heard at the Shrewsbury Quarter Sessions in April 1583 had a direct connection with the Sidney household. A certain James Lloyd, described as a servant of Sir Henry, was accused of counterfeiting the Lord President's name and handwriting. Unfortunately it is not recorded what the exact nature of this forgery was, but the very fact that James Lloyd was capable of writing suggests that he was a fairly senior figure amongst the servants of Sir Henry's household. Literacy rates are notoriously difficult to calculate, but the rate in provincial Elizabethan England is generally accepted as being between ten per cent to twenty per cent for males (the rate for females was much lower due to lack of educational opportunities for women at the time); the ability to read and write remained very much the exception rather than the rule. It is therefore likely that Lloyd was not a mere domestic servant but rather a steward of Sir Henry's household, responsible for the day-to-day management of the household finances and running costs.

It may be that Lloyd held a trusted position with regard to Sir Henry's presidency of the Council of the Marches; he may have been one of the numerous clerks employed to manage the finances of the Council. By this time Sir Henry Sidney himself appears to have fallen upon hard times; a letter written by him to Sir Francis Walsingham (his son's father-in-law) on 1 March 1583 survives, in which Sir Henry describes himself as 'having not so much grain as will feed a mutton', as being 'toothless and trembling' – he was only fifty-four at the time – and '£5,000 in debt'. There is no suggestion that Sir Henry had anything to do with James Lloyd's forgery of his signature, but the coincidence is intriguing. The letter from Sidney appears to have worked, as Sir Francis took on the debts of Sir Henry's son, Philip, when the latter became his son-in-law.

It is likely that Lloyd's case was heard at Shrewsbury Castle, which had become the main venue for Shropshire Quarter Sessions by the middle of the sixteenth century, and remained as such until 1712. Lloyd was brought up before the magistrates who, after hearing the details of the case, found him guilty as charged. Although details are sparse, it would appear that the specific nature of his document counterfeiting must have been fairly modest in its nature as his case was heard and sentenced there and then, as opposed to being sent for trial at the next Assizes.   Forgery (including counterfeiting of documents or currency) was theoretically a capital offence until 1832, and many forgers did indeed pay the ultimate penalty for their misdeeds.

Regardless of this, Lloyd must have bitterly regretted being caught, as his punishment was still a very painful affair. He was ordered to be taken from his place of confinement to the pillory which stood in Shrewsbury Market Square, where he was stripped to the waist and publicly flogged. The pillory consisted of hinged

Shrewsbury Castle Great Hall, site of Shropshire Quarter Sessions until 1712. The Author

wooden boards with holes through which the unfortunate individual's head and arms would be inserted. The hinged boards would then be fastened together. As the captive could neither move his head nor defend himself with his hands the pillory could be a very dangerous, even fatal, punishment dependent upon the mood of the crowd that invariably gathered to watch the suffering of the offender. If the crowd was hostile to the offender, stones and bricks could be thrown with serious results; there are numerous accounts of men being killed by missiles that hit them whilst they were imprisoned in the pillory. Equally so, if the mood of the crowd was sympathetic to the person being pilloried, the sentence could backfire, with cheering and even collections being made for the victim. There is no evidence that Lloyd was pelted with objects, but being pilloried was not the worst of his punishment, as it was also decreed that his ear was to be nailed to a board whilst the whipping took place. This would have added considerably to the discomfort felt by Lloyd as his natural inclination to twist his body to dodge the strokes of the whip would have greatly exacerbated the pain in his ear. Although not peculiar to Shropshire, this painful addition to the punishment of the pillory was used fairly frequently in the county – in February 1537 Sir Henry's predecessor, Bishop Lee, had written a letter making reference to its widespread practice in the local area.

As has been shown in the previous case, physical punishment of offenders (both male and female) could be extremely brutal in the medieval period and this situation continued throughout the early-modern period – for example, burning at the stake was not formally abolished until 1790, a year after a woman had been subjected to this form of torture. The pillory was used until 1837, whilst another popular form of punishment, the stocks, remained on the statute books as a punishment until 1872, although they were not in fact used much after the mid-nineteenth century. Those at Much Wenlock Guildhall were last recorded in use in 1852, when a Thomas Lloyd (no known relation of James Lloyd) was their final occupant.

Branding was a punishment that visibly marked felons or thieves with a permanent reminder that the offender had been found guilty of a criminal act. Thieves were normally branded with a 'T', felons with an 'F' and murderers with an 'M'. The location of the brand was normally on the thumb of the left hand, but for a brief period

An eighteenth-century revolving pillory at Newgate, London – note the considerable crowd and the armed guard around the pillory – possibly to protect the unwilling (and surprisingly well-dressed) participant from further harm. Author's collection

in the early eighteenth century it took place on the cheek. This was discontinued after 1707 as such branding prevented ex-offenders from gaining employment, as their previous misdemeanours were all too obvious for everyone to see. The use of branding or burning in any form as a punishment was not finally removed from the statute books until 1823, after ceasing in practice from 1799 (with the exception of the armed forces, where branding of deserters with a 'D' was not abolished until 1871, as a result of the reforms of the then Secretary of State for War, Edward Cardwell). Whipping or flogging remained one of the most commonly used methods of corporal punishment throughout the eighteenth and early nineteenth centuries. Public flogging of women stopped in 1817 and of men in 1862, but the private flogging of men continued until the middle of the twentieth century, being finally abolished in 1948 by the Criminal Justice Act of that year (private flogging in the Army had been abolished in 1881).

James Lloyd, when languishing in the pillory and probably bitterly regretting his decision to forge documents, would undoubtedly have done well to heed the advice written by his master Sir Henry to his son Philip, when he exhorted the young aristocrat (then at school in Shrewsbury) to 'be humble and obedient to your masters, for unless you frame yourself to obey others, yea, and feel in yourself what obedience is, you shall never be able to tell others to obey you.'

An unusual set of moveable stocks, Much Wenlock Guildhall – the last unwilling occupant being Thomas Lloyd in 1852. The Author

Chapter 3

'A foul-smelling foul deed'
Erection of an illegal 'house of office'
Hope Bowdler
1772

*This chapter shows that foul deeds could occasionally have their
humorous elements – the illegal erection in 1772 of a 'House of Office' –
a privy or toilet – near the King's Highway also highlights the fact that
the disposal of human excrement seems to have caused many problems
for the inhabitants of medieval and early-modern England.*

he disposal of human waste material has exercised the imagination
of people for many thousands of years, with the Romans
being one of the first civilizations to successfully address
the problems with an engineering solution. The
impressive remains at Viroconium (Wroxeter, near
Shrewsbury), the fourth largest town in Roman Britain, include
communal public toilets which had a supply of fresh running water

Remains of the latrines at Wroxeter (Viroconium) showing part of the drainage system.
The Author

channelled to flush away the contents of the latrines. The ingenious Romans also solved the problem of the lack of toilet tissue by the judicious issue of a sponge on a stick to each user of the latrine, which would be cleansed in a stream of water running through the building. A similar solution with regard to latrines was utilized by many medieval monastic communities, including Haughmond Abbey, which boasted an eighteen-seat communal facility, again replete with seats and running water.

Medieval royalty or aristocracy was often served by a slightly different solution; many castles or fortified houses were defended by water-filled moats, and these were also used as a convenient disposal place via long chutes or drops that emanated from garderobes (small private rooms containing a basic latrine – usually a stone seat with a conveniently shaped hole) built into the walls of towers. Ludlow Castle retains a magnificent suite of such facilities in its Garderobe Tower. Although these obviously removed the source of any smell or contamination from the immediate vicinity, one shudders to think of the state of the water in the moat. Hampton Court Palace similarly contained a 'Great House of Easement', which consisted of a two-storey building with a dividing wall modestly separating men's facilities from those of women.

However well-designed these latrines were, the problem of hygienically disposing of waste material remained a significant impediment to the general health of the population. The problem was by no means confined to the less well-off section of the community – even the rich and the famous had reason to lament the often appalling situation with regard to sanitation. By the middle of the seventeenth century some private houses were built with their own individual earth-closet or 'house of office', as they were euphemistically known, which went a limited way to mitigating the problem.

Unfortunately, these could cause occasionally pressing and indeed pungent problems to the occupiers of such houses and their neighbours. On 20 October 1660 Samuel Pepys, the most noted diarist of his age, recorded a memorable (though not oft-quoted) entry in his diary:

On going into my cellar, I put my foot into a great heap of turds, by

> *which I find that Mr Turner's house of office is full and comes into my cellar, which doth trouble me.*

Such unfortunate unsanitary incidents were the source of humour to both illustrators and writers throughout the seventeenth and eighteenth centuries, with a best-selling book containing often extremely bawdy (and occasionally downright obscene) examples of 'house of office' or 'bog-house' graffiti. *The Merry Thought or the Glass Window and Bog-House Miscellany*, first published c. 1731, ran to several volumes and numerous editions.

Memorably described as being 'the opposite to good taste', the book was published anonymously, but some literary historians have

Samuel Pepys (1633-1703), victim of an unfortunate accident in 1660. Author's collection

Brisk Cathartic *by James Gillray (1803), illustrating both a typical house of office and the often surprisingly quick effects of a powerful laxative!* Author's collection

THE
MERRY-THOUGHT:
OR, THE
Glafs-Window and Bog-Houfe
MISCELLANY.

Taken from

The Original Manufcripts written in *Diamond* by Perfons of the firft Rank and Figure in *Great Britain ;* relating to Love, Matrimony, Drun-kennefs, Sobriety, Ranting, Scandal, Politicks, Gaming, and many other Subjeƈts, *Serious* and *Comical.*

Faithfully Tranfcribed from the Drinking-Glaffes and Windows in the feveral noted *Taverns*, *Inns*, and other *Publick Places* in this Nation. Amongft which are intermixed the Lucubrations of the polite Part of the World, written upon Walls in Bog-houfes, *&c.*

Publifhed by HURLO THRUMBO.

Gameyorum, Wildum, Gorum,
Gameyorum a Gamy,
Flumarum a Flumarum,
A Rigdum Bollarum
A Rigdum, for a little Gamey.
Bethleham-Wall, Moor-Fields.

The THIRD EDITION ; with very Large Additions and Alterations.

LONDON:

Printed for J. ROBERTS in *Warwick-Lane*; and Sold by the Bookfellers in Town and Country.   [Price 6 *d.*]

Frontispiece of The Merry Thought, or the Glass Window & Bog-House Miscellany. Author's collection linked its authorship with Dr Samuel Johnson. It included the following scabrous remarks allegedly found on a house of office wall in Ludlow concerning a pair of unscrupulous peers and their adventures whilst attending the Races:

> *Two pitiful dukes at our races did appear,*
> *One bespoke him a girl, the other new gear,* ★
> *And both went away without paying, I hear,*
> *For the cheat loved his money, and so did the peer!*

★ an eighteenth-century slang word for stolen goods.

Other less than tasteful ditties included the following rhyming couplet:

> *If a man should breathe backward, and happen to stink,*
> *You may say, if you will, it is natural instinct.*

And, on 'a Person of Quality's Bog-House':

> *Good Lord! Who would think*
> *That such fine folks should stink!*

Human waste material could also be turned to profitable advantage in other ways than simply being the source of humorous publications. From the Roman period until the twentieth century stale human urine, which contained high levels of ammonia, was used extensively in several industrial processes. These included the fulling of cloth, tanning of leather, manufacture of saltpetre (used in the production of gunpowder), and, from Elizabethan times onward, the creation of alum, which was much-utilized as a colour stabilizer in the dyeing process. There were organized collectors of such material, with large receptacles placed on the street-corners of large towns and cities for both public and profitable convenience. Daniel Colwall, scientist and treasurer of the Royal Society, stated in his 1678 account of the English alum works that 'the best urine is that which comes from labouring people who drink little strong drink' – this was because strong alcohol upset the acidity level of the urine.

It is not clear whether or not the case that came before Shropshire magistrates at the Shrewsbury Quarter Sessions in

January 1772 was due to a desire to profit out of an everyday need or if the defendant considered that he was performing a public service. The surviving Quarter Sessions Rolls (a record of the proceedings of the quarterly magistrates' court held at Shrewsbury Guildhall) contain a True Bill (meaning that the magistrates considered that there was a prima facie case to answer) that was sworn in court by Edward Acton, Justice of the Peace, stating that:

> *John Croxton, a labourer of Hope Bowdler, with force and arms at the parish aforesaid, in or near the King's Highway, there did erect, put, and place, or cause to be erected, put, or placed a certain building called a Bog House, or House of Office, for the reception of dung, human excrement, and other filth, by which diverse hurtful, disagreeable and unwholesome smells from the said dung, excrement, and other filth, did then and there arise, and thereby the air there became and was greatly corrupted and infected to the great danger and common nuisance of all the liege subjects of our sovereign lord, the King, in, by, and through the King's Highway, returning, passing, riding and walking, and against the peace of our said lord, the King, his crown and dignity.*

Research carried out by members of www.hopebowdler.org.uk (a

Hope Bowdler. The Author

website dedicated to the history of the village) has shown that a Mr John Croxton lived in the parish of St Andrews, Hope Bowdler, from c.1716 to 1805. He served as churchwarden of St Andrews for over six decades, and as such was an important member of the local community, with his family gravestone being set into the outside wall of the church. There is no definitive confirmation available that this is the same John Croxton as the individual charged at Shrewsbury Quarter Sessions in 1772, but to have two people of the same forename and surname in a small village seems unlikely (there could of course be a father and son with the same name, as there is a considerable number of members of the extended Croxton family buried in the churchyard).

It is not clear whether the House of Office erected by Mr Croxton was a private facility or a public convenience, and unfortunately there is no survival of the verdict of the court – it is however unlikely that the case reached the Assizes, as it would have been considered a misdemeanor rather than a felony. Neither is there any record of any sentence handed out to the defendant (many of the Quarter Sessions records are believed to have been lost when the Shire Hall fell victim to a fire in 1883). However, it seems unlikely that Mr Croxton (much in the manner of anyone unfortunate enough to be in the vicinity of the illegally erected House of Office) would have emerged from his appearance in court smelling of roses!

It was not until the passing of the Public Health Act of 1848 that every dwelling in Britain was required by statute law to have access to a sanitary facility, be it earth-closet, ash-pit, privy or even replete with running water. Public and private sanitation continued to exercise the minds of people in Shropshire however, with a riot breaking out in Market Drayton in September 1868 following measures proposed by the wealthier inhabitants of the town to improve the provision of sanitary facilities. There was widespread opposition to the increasing number of private water closets proposed by the scheme, as they were thought to be a danger to public health because they flushed dirty water and waste material into the town's sewerage system, unlike the earth-closets that ensured that the waste material remained self-contained. A vote was held at the Corbet Arms Hotel on the measures to 'improve'

St Andrew's Parish Church, Hope Bowdler. John Croxton's gravestone is set into the wall immediately to the left of the porch. The Author

the sewers, and the *Shrewsbury Chronicle* reported that 'the vote led to as wild and extraordinary riot as has ever taken place in any spot in England'.

After an attempt by the wealthier inhabitants to force through acceptance of the new sanitary measures, a riot ensued, lasting for two days and necessitating the drafting-in of a considerable number of police constables from outside the town. Even this did not prove a strong enough deterrent, and the Market Drayton magistrates were forced to call in a detachment of soldiers from Manchester. The soldiers were from 64 Foot Regiment and numbered over sixty. Over forty men and women were arrested as a result, with many serving prison sentences of up to nine months as a result of their actions.

Although flushing toilets had been utilized by the wealthy few since the 1820s, it was not until the mid-twentieth century, following the developments and improvements made in the Victorian period by such sanitary engineers as the wonderfully named Thomas Crapper that the modern flushing toilet, directly served by mains water and connected to the public sewage system, became a common convenience in private homes.

Chapter 4

'Bank rags and worthless tokens' Counterfeiting in Halesowen 1818

This chapter illustrates the chaotic state of coinage in Britain as a result of the long wars fought with Napoleon, and shows the often ingenious means to which dedicated forgers and utterers of counterfeited coins would resort in order to make a nefarious profit. The case also highlights the machinations of judicial court procedure in the early nineteenth century, with one of the main protagonists turning king's evidence in order to evade a prison sentence.

During the social and economic upheaval of the Napoleonic wars the Bank of England faced a crisis with regard to a shortage of small denomination currency throughout Britain. The bank had been founded in 1694 as the first public bank in Britain, with the Bank of Scotland being founded in the following year. Their respective success led to the flourishing of provincial or 'country' banks throughout Britain. The number of country banks in England and Wales increased by over 224 per cent in the period 1793-1830, and this, together with the introduction of paper currency from 1797 in a somewhat futile effort to alleviate a shortage of coinage, led to a huge increase in forgery cases.

Forgery in the form of counterfeiting increased dramatically in the years following the suspension of payment in gold by the Bank of England in 1797; the Bank simply did not possess enough gold to honour its pledge to redeem its paper notes. The subsequent paper notes issued in lieu of gold by the Bank proved often irresistible to forgers, causing one caustic anonymous correspondent to write to the Bank in 1809 suggesting that every time a forgery was discovered, a Bank of England director should be publicly hanged. This, contended the writer, would rapidly improve note design and quality of printing – but not surprisingly the suggestion was not put into practice!

The *Report of the Constabulary Force Commissioners of 1839* stated that between 1805 and 1823 there were some 263,990 forged notes in circulation, and it has also been estimated that during this period as many as two-thirds of circulating coins were forged – causing one commentator to refer to notes and coins as 'bank rags and worthless tokens'. The Government had attempted to rectify the situation with regard to coinage in 1804, when on 8 March of that year the Privy Council requested blank dollars of Spanish silver to be stamped by the entrepreneurial industrialist Matthew Boulton of Birmingham and circulated at 5s. value (i.e. higher than the 4s. 6d. value of the silver content of the coin). By May 1804 such dollars were being stamped at the Soho Mint in Handsworth. The *Manchester Guardian* of 12 May 1804 reported that:

> *the new coinage of crown pieces from Dollars is now going on with all possible dispatch, at Mr Boulton's manufactory, the Soho, near Birmingham. Within these few days three waggons loaded with dollars were sent from the Bank, under a proper escort, to that place, each waggon contains about seven tons weight.*

The 'proper escort' seems to have been a contingent of Bow Street 'Runners', presumably accompanied by armed guards.

The costs of detecting and catching the counterfeiters could also be considerable. It has been estimated that in 1820 alone the Bank of England spent over £50,000 on prosecution and investigation of forgery. Two brief examples show the often large costs involved in such investigations. Firstly, in 1779 a forgery investigation carried out by two Bank of Scotland employees is recorded as reaching a total cost of £56 16s. 7d. Successful prosecution of the case cost a total of £128 17s. 11d., justice obviously coming at a high price in this instance. Secondly, an investigation of a forgery case at Cockermouth in 1812 carried out on behalf of Freshfield's, the Bank of England's solicitors, cost the Bank over £93 for the services of Freshfield's investigator Mr Christian and his deputy. These amounts may seem trivial in comparison to today's currency, but to reach a rough comparison of contemporary values it is

The New Coinage *by James Gillray (1817) – a satirical cartoon lampooning the Bank of England's attempts to rectify the nationwide shortage of small change.* Author's collection

necessary to multiply the figures by a factor of at least 100; therefore £50,000 equates to a modern amount of some £5,000,000.

From 1811-1813 the Bank made further attempts to alleviate the problem by introducing Bank Tokens in both one shilling and three shillings and sixpence denominations – in a similar manner to the stamped Spanish dollars, these tokens had a face value greater than that of their metal content. The tokens totalled a face value of £1,919,556 18s. 6d. Unfortunately the situation with regard to the provision of small denomination continued to worsen throughout the Napoleonic wars and it was widely reported that 'such Bank tokens invariably disappeared after their first circulation'. Britain's national debt rose to £850 million in 1815, and the shortage of coins, combined with a general economic downturn following the return of some 1/2 million demobbed soldiers and sailors, all of whom were looking for civilian employment, led to many people taking serious risks in order to turn a quick profit.

On 1 August 1818 Joseph Smith, a forty-one-year-old farmer from Halesowen, William Phillips senior, a fifty-year-old steel toymaker of Birmingham, and William Phillips junior, his twenty-year-old shoemaker son, appeared at Shrewsbury Assizes charged with high treason against the Crown by dint of 'counterfeiting the current coin of the realm' at Houghmore, in the parish of Halesowen, Shropshire.

As much of evidence in the trial was circumstantial in nature, Sir William Owen, counsel to the Royal Mint, which was normally the prosecuting agency in such coining trials, had refused to pay the considerable prosecution expenses, and had expressed a wish that the trial was not to be proceeded with. This viewpoint was heavily censured by both the Grand Jury and the judge, who stated that the expenses of the trial would be met either from the statutory rewards available in such trials or from the County Rate (local taxes).

The Grand Jury was a group which met at the beginning of the Assizes of every county in order to decide which trials were 'true bills' i.e. which should be proceeded with – in a similar manner to today's Crown Prosecution Service. The Grand Jury was made up of the 'great and the good' of the county, and the Shropshire Grand Jury of August 1818 was chaired by Lord Viscount Clive, who severely criticized the stance of the Royal Mint in this instance. The 'true' bills would then be brought to trial at the Assizes before a Petty Jury consisting of twelve men from a lower social (but still propertied) background than those of the Grand Jury. This system, which was not formally abolished until 1933, thereby 'performed a sifting function', but had very little professional legal expertise available to it when establishing whether or not cases were likely to succeed.

The Houghmore referred to in the trial report is in fact Uffmoor, a small rural settlement near Halesowen. The medieval town of Halesowen and its immediate environs was originally a detached part of the county of Shropshire and remained so until 1844, when it was transferred into the surrounding county of Worcestershire, later becoming part of the West Midlands administrative area.

Joseph Smith was a farmer residing at Uffmoor House. At the trial he admitted king's evidence; i.e. he became a witness for the prosecution in return for an implied offer of a greatly reduced sentence or pardon. He stated to the court that a couple of years ago two people named Bradley and Newnham asked to rent an upper room and cellar in his farmhouse. He agreed, and the two men then brought a nine-foot-long iron machine into his cellar which he since knew to be a press for the purpose of producing counterfeit coins. Bradley and Newnham carried on their illegal practices in the cellar for about a year until Newnham died at Michaelmas (29 September 1816).

The following Christmas, Bradley removed all their goods from Smith's farmhouse with the exception of the press. Smith stated that he had not laid eyes on Bradley since, but in the following September William Phillips senior visited Smith, stating that he knew Bradley and that he had been transported as a felon. The person in question was probably John Bradley, who was convicted at Warwick Assizes and transported for seven years on 1 April 1817, and who is recorded as serving his sentence in New South Wales and then somewhat ironically being appointed a constable on 16 June 1824 in Bringelly (a small settlement near Sydney). Bradley seems quickly to have returned to previous form however; he was dismissed from his post on 21 October 1825 for gross neglect of duty.

Halesowen, a detached part of Shropshire until 1844. The Author

Phillips senior then agreed terms with Smith to take over the rent of the cellar and the use of the press. Phillips and his son came to Uffmoor Farm during the following April and began operating the press. The cellar's window was blocked up with the exception of a small hole for ventilation. Smith visited the press in operation on one occasion and stated that the operation was very quick, with forged pieces being struck in a matter of seconds.

The existence of the press was also corroborated by a neighbour of Smith's, Anne Walker, who had visited Uffmoor Farm in April 1818 to borrow some bread. She stated that she heard a noise in the cellar and on closer inspection, she saw two men hard at work on the press. She positively identified William Phillips senior and junior as the operators of the press. It seems that word of the illegal press had leaked out to a wider audience, as Joseph Smith junior, son of the farmer, testified that in early May 1818 he had been asked to give a message to his father from William Phillips senior that 'a screw was loose'; in other words the game was up, and that Phillips intended to remove the press to nearby Brierley Hill in Staffordshire. Joseph Smith senior seems to have panicked at this news, and instructed his son to bury the flywheel of the press in a field on 7 May.

Smith's fears were well-founded, as the Chief Constable of the Division of Halesowen, Joseph Grainger, paid a visit to Uffmoor Farm on 9 May as the result of a tip-off. He ostensibly searched the farm for some lost chickens, but soon discovered the press, together with some unstruck blanks, several forged three-shilling bank tokens and a forged one shilling-and-sixpence piece. Chief Constable Grainger took Smith into custody and then arrested the Phillips at their home in Sally Street, Birmingham.

Joseph Smith obviously decided that it was in his best interests to cooperate fully with the forces of law and order, and consequently voluntarily confessed all to the local magistrates, Mr William Woodcock, Mr Ferdinando Smith and Mr James Male, at their Halesowen court on 15 May 1818. Joseph Smith and the Phillips subsequently attended a hearing before Shrewsbury Quarter Sessions magistrates on 13 July 1818 and it was decided that there was enough evidence for the case to come before the forthcoming

Assizes. At his trial at the Shrewsbury Assizes held on 29 July 1818 Joseph Smith strongly denied knowing that there was a reward for convicting the other prisoners; he also refuted the claim that he knew he would escape punishment by turning king's evidence. *The Times* of 8 August 1818 carried the following statement by Smith:

> *I first gave information to Mr Woodcock on the 9th May last: I voluntarily confessed to him; I do not know, upon my honour (at this expression of witness there was an involuntary laugh in the Court), upon my word, upon my oath, that there is a reward for convicting the prisoners; I do not know that I shall be free from punishment by giving evidence to convict the prisoners; but I have been told by the elder prisoner, and before that I have heard such a thing said in my own country. I told the magistrate I would confess, before I knew I should be free for so doing.*

When questioned, Constable Joseph Grainger also strenuously denied knowing that there was a reward offered for the conviction of the Phillips; he stated that the elder Phillips had expressed a wish to turn king's evidence himself, and that he (Grainger) did not think himself entitled to any reward, 'nor had any such motive actuated his conduct'. There was clearly an attempt by the defence to insinuate that Grainger had been motivated by the thought of receiving a reward and that he may not have acted in a correct manner when arresting the prisoners. An expert witness in the shape of Mr Robert Morris, a silversmith from Shrewsbury, was called to give evidence as to the forged coins found at the press in Uffmoor. He also examined a forged shilling found on Phillips senior's person at the time of his arrest. He opined that the forged coins found at the press were illegally stamped, but that they were not in a finished condition – it appears that some of the coins did not possess milled edges, which they would need in order to pass as coins of the realm (see *Punch* cartoon below). He further deposed that the forged items would also have needed to be silvered again after being stamped in the press. Mr Morris's evidence concluded the case for the prosecution, and no witnesses were called on behalf of the prisoners, although they did apparently have a defence counsel, Mr Hart. This was fairly unusual in the early nineteenth century; the majority of trials took place without the prisoner having access to a professional lawyer, to whom they would have had to have paid a considerable fee. The role of barristers in criminal courts was to blossom spectacularly throughout the first half of the nineteenth century: *Law Review* figures show that in 1809 there were only 456 practising barristers in England, compared to a total of over 3,000 by 1846.

In his summing-up the judge cautioned the jury that they must not base their evidence on Smith's testimony alone, but must weigh the other evidence before reaching their verdict, as two men's lives depended on their judgement. He also stressed the judiciousness of the prosecution in basing its case on the operation of the die, as the unfinished forgeries found in the prisoners' possession or at the site of the press could not have sustained a trial in their own right as they were not in a state to be passed as coins of the realm. Neither could the trial have been founded on the possession of the press, as it was not clear which of the Phillips owned the machine. The jury seems to have made its mind up quickly however, and within a matter of minutes after retiring they returned a verdict of 'guilty' against both the Phillips. The judge seems to have been extremely conscientious, and instead of sentencing the men there and then – and if it had been a straightforward case they would probably have been condemned to death, as forgery was theoretically a capital offence until 1832 (with the last hanging for forgery occurring in 1829) – he instead decided to put the case before the Twelve Judges (Law Lords) in the House of Lords, the most senior justices in the land. Judgement against the prisoners was therefore respited and they were remanded in custody until the next Assizes, when sentence would be passed. The judge did however caution both prisoners against indulging in any hopes of mercy, as the offence of high-treason was an extremely serious one.

Surviving records are sketchy as to what eventual fate befell Phillips senior and junior. The Calendar of Prisoners for the Summer Assize of 1818 (a printed record of those appearing before Quarter Sessions magistrates and Assize judges, produced shortly after each Quarter Session or Assize) states that judgement in their case was indeed respited and that they were not sentenced to death, but to a sentence of seven years' transportation to Australia. Subsequent Calendars do not show them remaining in custody,

Omnibus conductor: "Look 'ere – this arf-crown won't do. It ain't got no milling*
on its hedge." Passenger: "Blimey! Nor it 'as! I knew I'd forgotten somefink!"
Cartoon from Punch, or the London Charivari, *25 August 1920, showing the*
results of a poorly executed forgery.
*milling – the provision of ridges on the edges of coins of the realm – was originally
introduced to counter the practice of 'clipping' coins, whereby the edges of coins were
clipped in order to obtain small off-cuts of silver or gold which could then be melted
down. Author's collection

which would suggest that they were indeed transported. Searches
in the 1841 census (the earliest available) confirm that neither
Phillips senior or junior appear in the surviving records, again

suggesting that they were sent overseas. However, it has not been possible to trace them in Australian convict records, and it is possible that they instead served out their sentences on a prison hulk (floating prisons created out of rotting former warships – these were first utilized in 1776 to deal with the ever-increasing number of convicts, and continued in use until the 1850s). Conditions aboard these disease-infested wrecks were often seen as worse than those experienced by transportees in Australia. However, if the Phillips did serve out their sentences on such a ship, they should still have been recorded in the 1841 census, so their actual fate remains a mystery.

Joseph Smith seems to have been an extremely lucky individual in escaping any form of legal censure as a result of his turning king's evidence. In the years following his appearance at Shrewsbury Assizes he seems to have learned the error of his ways and concentrated on farming. In the 1841 census he is listed as living at Uffmoor Farm with his wife and several children, together with four live-in agricultural labourers. In 1851 he is described as being a farmer of 110 acres, employing three labourers and a domestic servant. No doubt in his later life (and he lived well into his seventies) he occasionally reflected upon his brush with the law with a sigh of relief.

Counterfeiting of both coins and notes of the realm continued to be a serious problem during the first two decades of the nineteenth centuries, but from 1817 counterfeiters found it increasingly difficult to forge used coins, as in that year the Royal Mint recalled all official silver coinage and issued new coins that were more difficult to copy. However, as the *Punch* cartoon shows, the problem of counterfeited coins continued well into the twentieth century, and indeed forged bank notes still pose a serious problem in the twenty-first century.

Chapter 5

'Of all the murders that ever was heard of, this is the most shocking' Infanticide in Bridgnorth 1823

This chapter illustrates a particularly brutal murder of a defenceless and innocent infant by his stepfather, and also shows how easy it was in the early nineteenth century to obtain poisonous substances. The length of murder trials and the swift imposition of justice is also notable.

On the last Monday in September 1823, a coroner's inquest held at Bridgnorth heard how an infant, Richard Overfield, had been killed by oil of vitriol poisoning. The jury quickly reached a verdict of 'Wilful Murder' against the child's father, also called Richard Overfield. These events were the start of an investigation into one of the most shocking murders in Shropshire during the nineteenth century.

In the early 1800s carpet weaving was developed as a new industry in Bridgnorth by the McMichael family of nearby Kidderminster; the *Handbook to the Severn Valley Railway*, published in 1863, stated that 'two carpet manufactories were established there about 1810'. The ventures proved successful, and although Kidderminster retained its pre-eminence in the industry throughout the nineteenth century, Bridgnorth was also a recognized centre of the production of quality carpets – even fulfilling orders from royalty and producing a special carpet for Queen Victoria's Golden Jubilee in 1887. In 1824 the McMichael's factory was joined by Southwell's in Friar Street, and between them the two firms employed a considerable percentage of the Bridgnorth workforce.

Amongst the workforce of McMichael's was a young man named

Richard Overfield. He had been born in Bridgnorth, being christened 11 February 1787, the son of Edward and Elizabeth Overfield. He worked for several years as a labourer assisting in the process of washing worsted yarns. He earned eleven shillings a week in 1823 (a fairly average wage for a labourer at the time), and was described by the factory superintendent, Mr Thomas Ross Southwell, as 'a quiet, hard-working, peaceable man'. However, despite Richard's steady employment and apparent good character, his home life appears to have been a deeply unhappy one. In the summer of 1823 he married Anne, who at the time was pregnant with a child that was not Richard's. It appears that Richard had agreed to marry Anne at the request of Bridgnorth parish officials, who were keen to avoid the cost of another illegitimate child on the local poor rate. He seems to have been offered (and accepted) a sum of money in return for saving the parish the cost of raising the child, as a child born more than a month after a marriage was deemed legitimate, and therefore Richard became liable for the child's upkeep.

The child was christened Richard (probably indicating a desire by the mother to announce its legitimacy to the world) on 10 August 1823. However, there seems to have been absolutely no step-paternal feelings on the elder Richard's part; he was heard to frequently express a hatred for the infant and on several occasions was reported as stating that he would not support his wife or her 'bastard child'.

Matters came to a tragic head on the morning of Sunday, 21 September 1823, when between 11am and midday Louisa Davies, a neighbour of the Overfields, heard Anne Overfield screaming loudly. Louisa rushed round to the Overfields, where she found Anne cradling her three-month-old son in her arms. Anne put the child's mouth to hers and tasted his lips. She said that something in the child's mouth tasted hot, sour and bitter, and made her mouth smart. Clearly suspecting her husband of foul play, Anne turned to Richard, saying 'O Dick, Dick! What have you done to my child?' He calmly replied 'Nothing at all, my wench: but the black cat got up to the child's mouth and brought foam up, and I knocked it off.'

A distraught Anne rushed with the critically-ill baby to the house of the local surgeon, Mr Joseph Hall, and saw his assistant, Mr

Edward John Spry. She was at first unable to tell Mr Spry what had happened because of her very distressed state, but finally managed to ask him to taste the child's mouth. He did so, noting that the baby's lips were white and shrivelled, with blisters on their inner surface. Spry diagnosed that the child had been poisoned as a result of swallowing oil of vitriol (now better known as sulphuric acid, one of the more powerful toxins). Mr Hall was called for his opinion, and the child was given suspended magnesia in water in order to neutralize the acid, together with gruel and barley water. Despite these efforts (which would not have had much effect on such a severe case of poisoning) the baby's condition continued to worsen, and at around 3pm on the same day he died. A coroner's inquest was hastily arranged, and Richard Overfield was subsequently arrested by the local amateur parish constable, Edward Goodall (Bridgnorth Borough Police force was not created until 1836).

As a result of the findings of the coroner and his jury, Overfield was committed for trial and remanded at Shrewsbury Gaol, but before the Assizes began, an indictment, together with any depositions that may have been taken, was submitted to the Grand Jury which decided that there was sufficient likelihood of the trial being successful and that a 'true bill' had been presented. Because the death of the infant had taken place in late September, only a month after the previous Shropshire Summer Assizes, Richard Overfield was remanded in prison at Shrewsbury County Gaol for almost six months until the start of the 1824 Lent Assizes in mid-March. During that time, he maintained his story that he had administered nothing to the child, but had simply found the family cat lying on top of the baby, impeding its breathing, and had consequently shooed it off. At his trial he pleaded 'not guilty' to the murder of his infant stepson.

The trial commenced on Friday, 19 March at Shrewsbury before Mr Justice Park, who was a well-known Assize judge who had only a few months previously presided at one the most infamous murder trials of the nineteenth century: the trial of John Thurtell for the brutal murder of William Weare in Hertfordshire. Sir James Alan Park (1763-1838) was known as an old-fashioned but capable judge, with an uncanny physical resemblance to King George III (of which he was apparently very proud). Judges were influential and propertied men; even *puisne* (lesser) judges were salaried at £3,000 per year in 1799 – this equates to around £300,000 in modern terms and was a far cry from the wages of most of those tried at the Assizes. Judges have always been well paid in an attempt to negate the possibility of bribery.

To present-day eyes, the judicial system of the early nineteenth century seems almost unbelievably biased against the defendant. Apart from the fact that the jury members were all propertied and consequently wealthy male individuals, and therefore can be seen as not being representative of the population as a whole, the defendant was only allowed a limited form of what would now be called legal aid in the defence of a murder charge. Whilst both prosecuting and defending counsel could call and cross-examine witnesses, until 1836 defence counsel was prohibited from summing up, and it was not until the passing of the Criminal Evidence Act in 1898 that defendants were allowed to give evidence on oath.

Despite Overfield's continued protestations of innocence, it soon transpired that the evidence against him was overwhelming. Louisa Davies was the first witness to be called, as in common law Anne Overfield could not give evidence on oath either for or against her husband. Another neighbour, Mary Nichols, was called by the prosecution and she stated that she lived immediately next door to the Overfields, on the side opposite to Louisa Davies. She said that from a window in her house overlooking the garden of the Overfields she had seen Richard Overfield walk down to the bottom of his garden and that 'when he was at the bottom he made a kind of stoop as he was turning, and went up again'. She stated that there was a hole in the paling (fence) where he had stooped, and that she subsequently pointed out the spot to Louisa Davies. Louisa confirmed Mary's story, and stated that the day after the death of the infant she went round to comfort Anne, who was feeling faint. Louisa took Anne for a walk round the garden to get some fresh air, and found a phial with a cork in it at the spot where Richard Overfield had been seen by Mary Nichols. She stated that the cork was black, with about a teaspoonful of liquid remaining in the phial.

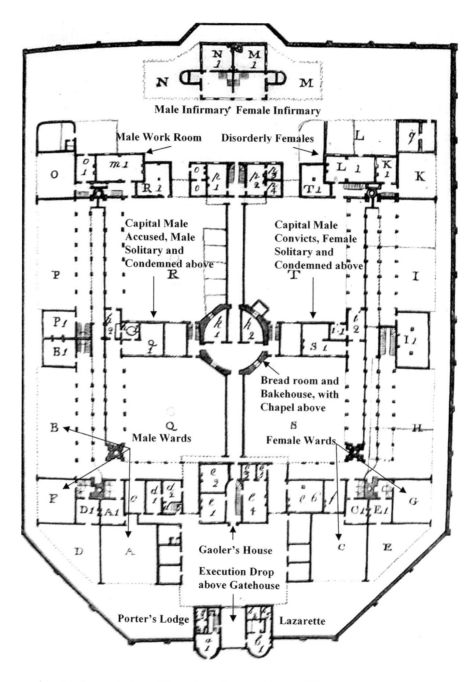

Annotated ground plan of Shrewsbury County Prison, 1797. (© Shropshire Archives)

She returned to the house and contacted Constable Goodall, who took the phial away.

The next witness was Thomas Ross Southwell, the superintendent at Overfield's place of work. He stated that oil of vitriol was used on a daily basis at the carpet factory, where it was utilized in the dyeing process. He further stated that there was no way that Overfield could have failed to notice that such poisonous material was used at the factory. Southwell reported that he found it surprising that Overfield reported for work as normal the day after the death of the child, and that he (Southwell) had enquired about what had happened. Overfield repeated his version of events to Southwell, and showed no emotion at the news that there would have to be a coroner's inquest. Southwell reported him as saying 'Let them open it, and then they will see'. Significantly, Southwell also stated that the room containing the oil of vitriol was often left unattended, with the key in the door.

Constable Goodall was the next witness for the prosecution, and he stated that he delivered the phial to Mr Hall the surgeon, who poured three drops out of it and returned it to the constable. Goodall also recalled that the day that Richard Overfield was due to be taken to Shrewsbury his wife came to see him and asked him to confess before God. Overfield replied 'I have the truth at my tongue's end, but I dare not speak it. My dear wench, you have got my watch; keep it for my sake, as I shall never come back, and give my clothes to my poor old father'. Dr Dugard, a physician practising in Shrewsbury, was called in his professional capacity, and he dismissed categorically Overfield's explanation regarding the choking of the child by the family cat. He stated that the death of the baby was undoubtedly caused by its imbibing oil of vitriol.

The defence counsel called several of the witnesses back for cross-examination, but Richard Overfield contributed very little to his own defence. He had objected to three jury members at the start of his trial (as was his right – he may have thought that the pre-trial publicity of the case had influenced some of the jurors), but when asked to make his defence, he merely repeated that he was innocent of the crime. The trial lasted less than a day (not unusual in early nineteenth-century trials, many of which lasted a matter of minutes rather than hours), and the jury took less than five minutes to bring in a unanimous verdict of 'guilty'. The judge then addressed the prisoner, stating that 'I have only one consolation as respects you – that you have been for six months in prison, and that you entered it with a conviction of the punishment which awaited your crime; and therefore I trust you have sought mercy where alone it can be granted. If not, let me implore you, for your soul's sake, to lose not a moment'. He then pronounced the sentence:

> *'that you be taken to the place from whence you came, and from thence, on Monday next, 22 March, to a place of execution, and there be hanged by the neck until you are dead; and that, after your death, your body be delivered to the surgeons to be anatomized, and may God have mercy on your soul'.*

Under the statutes of the 1752 Murder Act, no appeal was allowed (although requests for royal pardons were relatively commonplace), and sentence had to be carried out within forty-eight hours of the verdict (unless, as in Overfield's case, the sentence was passed on a Friday, whereby the hanging would take place on the following Monday, as it was not thought proper to carry out the death sentence on a Sunday). The death penalty by hanging was automatic at this time in such cases, and was also regularly imposed on many lesser felonies, there being over 200 crimes that carried a statutory death penalty at this time. Although the perceived merits of both what had become known as the Bloody Code and capital punishment in particular by this time were coming under some question, many contemporary defendants of this system agreed with Archdeacon William Paley, who in his *Principles of moral and political philosophy* (1785) had argued that 'the end of punishment was not justice. It was deterrence – and deterrence through terror'. He also argued that if the wrong man was occasionally hanged by mistake, then the unfortunate victim could be considered to have died for the greatest good.

The general perception of the condemned man or woman being allowed a hearty breakfast is a misguided and apocryphal one: Article VII of the 1752 Murder Act states that 'until the execution [...] such offender shall be fed bread and water only, and with no other food or liquor whatsoever'. There was also always the fear on the part of the authorities that friends or accomplices of the condemned may try to snatch them either before or after the sentence had taken place. To dissuade such individuals, the Murder Act made explicit the ferocity of the law should anyone be found guilty of such an action: attempts to rescue the condemned person before the sentence was carried out would result in the automatic death penalty, whilst cutting down the body of the condemned after hanging carried a sentence of seven years transportation. Similarly, a failed attempt at rescuing the body from the anatomists prior to dissection would also carry the penalty of seven years' transportation. Anatomical dissection was the normal means of disposing of the body of the hanged person; a Christian burial was not permitted in the hope that the fear of not being allowed to rest in consecrated ground would also act as an added deterrent to those considering a serious criminal act.

Public interest in trials such as Overfield's was considerable at both local and national levels. *Hanging Notices*, giving details of the date and time of the hanging, together with an often highly elaborated potted history of the case, were hurriedly printed and fly-posted outside the relevant gaol. They, along with the penny ballad sheets which often put the lurid and shocking details of the perpetrator's offences to the tune of a popular song of the moment, served to promote ghoulish and sensational interest among the general public. The printer of Overfield's *Last Dying Speech* was an enterprising individual, Mr Waidson, whose printing works was located in Dog Lane (now Claremont Street). He was responsible for many similar such printed sheets detailing the last speeches and confessions of condemned men and women. These were generally basically accurate, but also highly sensationalized, with a standard cheap woodcut print of the gallows, in order to attract a large number of buyers. As previously stated, literacy rates are notoriously difficult to ascertain, but current general consensus suggests that around two-thirds of the English population was literate to varying degrees by the second quarter of the nineteenth century. This accords with a table of convicts' literacy printed in the *Manchester Guardian* on 25 April 1838:

Hanging cell, Perth Gaol, Western Australia – a similar scene (although rather more public) would have faced Richard Overfield as he waited for his execution on the top of the gatehouse at Shrewsbury Gaol. The chair was for condemned prisoners who fainted or who were unable to stand on the trap-door due to fear. The Author

Convicts unable to read or write	35.85 %
Read and write imperfectly	52.08 %
Read and write well	9.46 %
Received superior instruction	0.43 %
Unknown standard	2.18 %

Richard Overfield apparently showed no emotion at the verdict and was led quietly away from the dock to his fate. At the time of his hanging, he apparently repented and confessed to the murder of his stepson. Infanticide was by no means uncommon in the nineteenth century; a conscientious Middlesex coroner, Edwin Lankester, who followed up many more cases of infant death than most of his colleagues, stated in 1862 that he considered there to be over 1,000 murders of children and infants in England and Wales each year, many of which were recorded as accidental death or death by natural causes.

This contrasts starkly with the official annual homicide (murder and manslaughter) figures of around 400 per year and suggests that many of these deaths were not fully investigated by either coroners or the police. However, the vast majority of infant murderers were women (overwhelmingly the mother of the child), and Richard Overfield's heartless crime seems to have particularly stirred the indignation of the local populace, with his printed 'confession and last dying speech' stating that 'of all the murders that ever was heard of, this is the most shocking'.

Chapter 6

'Brother appearing against brother, daughter against son, and son against mother' Murder in Market Drayton 1827

This chapter records a particularly vicious and premeditated foul deed, in which several members of an extended family were culpable of serious criminal behaviour. The case later drew the attention of Sir Arthur Conan Doyle, and also explodes the myth of 'honour among thieves'.

On the evening of 17 July 1827 James Harrison, a twenty-one-year-old petty thief, was called upon by a criminal acquaintance, Joseph Pugh. Pugh said that he and two further acquaintances, John Cox and his younger brother Robert, (no known relation! – author) were going to steal some bacon and required Harrison to assist them. Harrison agreed to accompany them on their nefarious mission, and the two men walked up to the junction of Mere Lane and Tinkers Lane, where they met John and Robert Cox. The unsuspecting Harrison was then set upon by Pugh, who knocked him down, and John Cox then strangled him with a garrotte made from a cheap cord and a stick. Robert Cox kept lookout whilst the foul deed was being perpetrated. The trio then hastily buried the body behind a haystack in a nearby field. They returned some time later and removed the body to a more secure grave in another field further away from the road.

Why did the three men cold-bloodedly murder James Harrison? Their motive was to remain a mystery for almost a year, and when it was discovered, it revealed a dastardly plot between several members of an extended family.

During the last week of June 1828, Thomas Ellson, a young man from Market Drayton, was being held by Drayton magistrates on a charge of fowl-stealing. During the course of his questioning by one of the Drayton magistrates, Mr Thomas Twemlow, Ellson stated that he had been previously arrested on suspicion of stealing potatoes and had been taken to Stafford Gaol on the day before Good Friday, 1827. He was then transferred to Shrewsbury Gaol, where he remained for three months awaiting trial at the next Shropshire Assizes, after further enquiries had implicated him as a member of a sheep-stealing gang that had operated in the Market Drayton area. Ellson had married the daughter of John Cox senior (the father of John and Robert Cox) and knew his brothers-in-law well. His mother was Ann Harris, who had given birth to Thomas by a previous husband. The chief witness for the prosecution in the forthcoming trial for sheep-stealing (then a capital offence) was a certain James Harrison.

Ellson's trial at the Summer Shropshire Assizes of 1827 collapsed due to lack of evidence; James Harrison did not appear to give evidence for the prosecution, as (obviously unknown to the

Scene of the callous murder of James Harrison in 1827. The Author

prosecution counsel) he was by then lying in a shallow grave some miles away in Hocknell's Field, Market Drayton. He had been murdered in order to keep him from giving evidence against Ellson that would almost undoubtedly have sent Ellson to the gallows.

At his examination before magistrates in late June 1828, in an attempt to obtain a pardon from his stealing offences, Ellson stated that he had been told of the murder of Harrison after his release from Shrewsbury Gaol. He had met the Cox family at the Star public house in Market Drayton, where he stated that Robert Cox had told him 'if it had not been for me and Joe Pugh, you would not have been here now'. The whole story was then recounted to him of how the Cox brothers and Joseph Pugh had lured Harrison from his lodgings and then murdered him at the behest of Ellson's mother, Ann Harris, and their father, John Cox senior.

Before the shocked magistrates, Ellson then stated that he knew where the body of Harrison was buried. A digging party was hastily convened and despatched to Hocknell's field. First attempts on 26 June 1828 to locate the body were unsuccessful, but three days later, as a consequence of Joseph Pugh confessing to the murder, he was taken to the field and was able to precisely point out the grave. Harrison's body was unearthed in a badly decomposed state, but positive identification was made possible at the coroner's inquest (held on 30 June 1828) by his clothes, as the body had not been stripped. The Cox brothers and father, along with Ann Harris, were then also taken into custody.

Following the coroner's inquest a verdict of 'wilful murder' was charged against John Cox senior (60), John Cox junior (26), Robert Cox (19), Joseph Pugh (19) and Ann Harris (50). The five suspects were then detained at Shrewsbury Gaol to await their trial at the next Assizes. Pugh's case was not helped by the revelation in the press that his elder brother, Robert, had been transported for life at Shrewsbury Assizes in March 1827 for highway robbery.

The trial of the five prisoners took place on Saturday, 2 August 1828 at Shrewsbury Assizes where the full facts of the murder were laid before the jury. Several witnesses gave evidence as to the last-known movements and whereabouts of James Harrison, and then Thomas Ellson was called to the stand. There was clearly no 'honour among thieves' in this case; Ellson was only too ready to sacrifice the lives of his mother and his in-laws in order to save his own skin. He stated that on the night he had been released from gaol Robert Cox had called round to his mother's house and, referring to the body of the murdered Harrison, said 'damn your old eyes, if you don't give me some more money, I'll fetch him and rear him up against thy door!' Ellson's mother gave Cox two shillings and told him not to bother her ever again.

It transpired that Ann Harris had been trying for some time to ensure that Harrison did not testify against her son. She had conversed with John Cox senior and prevailed upon him to buy some arsenic, by which means she intended to poison Harrison. John Cox senior had indeed tried to buy a penny-worth of arsenic from a Market Drayton druggist 'for a sick dog', but the suspicious druggist had refused to sell him any. Mrs Harris had also asked her sister-in-law to procure some arsenic for her, but she had refused.

An attorney, Mr Charles Warren, was next in the witness-box. He testified that Joseph Pugh had approached him on 28 June 1828 and said that he would tell all about the Harrison murder if Warren could save him. Mr Warren then stated that Pugh denied being present at the murder, but that he (Pugh) knew all the facts of the murder. Pugh finally admitted being part of the group that took part in Harrison's murder, but stated that he had just knelt on Harrison whilst John Cox junior had strangled him and Robert Cox had acted as lookout.

The next evidence heard was the written confession of Ann Harris. She confirmed that she had wanted Harrison to be killed and that she originally wanted him to be thrown down a coal-pit. She further admitted to asking several people to acquire arsenic for her to poison Harrison, and also provided a shovel for his grave to be dug. After the murder had taken place, she wanted the murderers to collect his body and throw it down a well in order that the foul deed would remain undiscovered. She also confessed to promising the murderers fifty shillings each for carrying out the killing.

The court next heard that rumours concerning the whereabouts of James Harrison had been spread by the Coxes in order to explain his absence – it was stated that he had joined a regiment in Wales and had been seen there recently. Robert Cox pleaded his innocence in the matter of the murder, whilst his father John stated that there was no evidence against him. He had wanted to call a witness for his defence, but had been advised against such action by his defence counsel. However, John appealed directly to the judge and his witness was called. In the event, he was unable to provide any new evidence that pointed to Cox senior's innocence.

After hearing all the evidence in the twelve-and-a-half-hour trial, the jury retired for a matter of minutes before returning a verdict of 'guilty' on all the prisoners. Judge Gasellee then addressed the prisoners, stating that John Cox junior, his brother Robert, and Joseph Pugh had been found guilty of murder, whilst John Cox senior and Ann Harris had been found guilty of being accessories before the fact of murder, and that all sentences carried the death penalty. Judge Gasellee further remarked:

> *The crime of murder at any time appals the heart of everyone; but no man, when he considers the circumstance of this murder, and that the object of it was to defeat the ends of justice, can hesitate to say that it is of a description unparalleled in the annals of crime.*

The judge then passed sentence of death on Pugh and the Cox brothers, ordering them to be executed on the following Monday, and that their bodies be subject to the usual fate of being given to the anatomists for dissection. The sentences on Ann Harris and John Cox senior were to be carried out a couple of weeks later. *The Times* concluded that:

> *This was altogether a most revolting case. Pugh, the father, was called to convict his own son, Ellson to convict his own mother and father-in-law, and brothers-in-law. His wife corroborated his evidence against her own father and brothers; and the evidence of Ann Harris' daughter, tended to confirm the testimony which fixed the guilt on her mother.*

At midday on Monday, 4 August 1828 Joseph Pugh and John Cox junior were hanged in front of a huge crowd at Shrewsbury Gaol. Robert Cox, who had continued to protest his innocence in the physical action of murdering James Harrison, had his sentence commuted to transportation for life. He was transported as convict 3202 to Van Diemen's Land (modern-day Tasmania) on the *Lady Harewood*, and seems to have become a somewhat reformed character.

He gained his parole in 1835 and a conditional pardon in 1840, having had 'only two trivial offences recorded against him' during his time in Australia. He must have considered himself extremely fortunate. John Cox senior was similarly lucky in that his death sentence was revoked – he had consistently denied any part in the murderous plan, despite Ann Harris' protestations that he was in fact the concocter of the idea. Ann Harris was one of almost 210 women to be publicly hanged in the British Isles between 1800 and 1868, when hanging began to take place within the private grounds of prisons. She was also the last woman to be publicly hanged at Shrewsbury.

The case again came to prominence some sixty years later, when Sir Arthur Conan Doyle, author of the Sherlock Holmes stories and an avid amateur detective, wrote a melodramatic (and somewhat inaccurate) short factual piece on the murder for *Chambers Journal*, entitled *The Bravoes of Market Drayton* (bravoes were hired killers or

Sir Arthur Conan Doyle.
Author's collection

assassins). In it he wrote that:

> *The traveller who in the days of our grandfathers was whirled through this beautiful region upon the box-seat of the Liverpool and Shrewsbury coach, was deeply impressed by the Arcadian simplicity of the peasants, and congratulated himself that innocence, long pushed out of the great cities, could still find a refuge amid these peaceful scenes. Most likely he would have smiled incredulously had he been informed that neither in the dens of Whitechapel* [scene of the Jack the Ripper murders in the winter of 1888] *nor in the slums of Birmingham was morality so lax or human life so cheap as in the fair region which he was admiring.*

In concluding his account of the brutal and calculated murder of James Harrison, he optimistically stated:

> *The air of the Shropshire downs was the sweeter for the dispersal of the precious band; and it is on record that this salutary example brought it home to the rustics that the law was still a power in the land, and that, looking upon it as a mere commercial transaction, the trade of the bravo was not one which could flourish upon English soil.*

Chapter 7

'As mad as a hatter?'
Theft of cows' tails in Osbaston
1830

This chapter shows that not all foul deeds in Shropshire were concerned with murder or serious felonies. The vast majority of criminal cases have always been relatively petty in nature and as such were heard before magistrates), rather than before Assize judges. This remains the situation today, with over 97 per cent of all criminal cases (some 1½ million cases per year) being heard before voluntary unpaid magistrates.

Many of the cases in this book, being serious in nature, were heard at the most senior of the provincial courts, namely the County Assizes, which were presided over by London-based judges, but this was not the usual procedure for the vast majority of criminal cases, which were heard before local magistrates.

By the beginning of the nineteenth century the duties of a magistrate had increased considerably, especially in the field of Poor Relief, and during the 'long' eighteenth century from the 'Glorious Revolution' of 1688 to the fall of Napoleon in 1815, the role of the magistracy of England underwent several fundamental changes, including a gradual but inexorable shift of workload from purely criminal cases to civil duties such as the maintenance of the poor, resettlement of vagrants and responsibility for ensuring that there was no flouting of Sunday trading laws. Throughout the period there was a transfer of power from the Crown and centralized government to the counties and local bodies. At the same time, other forms of local jurisprudence and social control had lost much of their former powers in the preceding century; manorial courts and parish vestries (which had formerly dealt with minor misdemeanours) often became largely honorific bodies – little more than a good excuse for an annual formal dinner. With regard to criminal cases, a flurry of legislation throughout the eighteenth century had also greatly increased magistrates' jurisdiction in summary matters.

Magistrates were appointed by the Crown after representations from the Lord Lieutenant of the respective county, and from the last quarter of the seventeenth century newly appointed magistrates had to swear oaths of allegiance to the king, the Protestant faith and the office of Justice of the Peace, and then authorize these oaths by taking out a writ of *mediums potentate* (literally 'we have given the power'). Such a series of oaths survives from 1738, in which John Bright, Esquire, swore the following in front of Maurice Pugh and Thomas Moore on his appointment as a Justice of the Peace:

I do hereby promise and swear that I will be faithful and bear true allegiance to his Majesty King George so help me God.

The oaths continued with Bright's hand still placed on the Bible, and after swearing to abhor, detest and abjure Catholicism (memories of the reign of King James II were still fresh in people's minds), he was then instructed that:

Ye shall swear that as Justice of the Peace in the county of Salop in all articled in the King's Commission to you directed ye shall do equal right to the poor and to the rich after your cunning wit and power; and after the Law and customs of this Realm and Statutes thereof made; and ye shall not be at counsel with any person in any quarrel hanging afore you; and that ye hold your Sessions after the form of Statutes thereof made; and that fines [which] shall happen to be made and all forfeitures which shall fall before you, ye shall truly cause to be entered without any concealment or embezzlement and truly send them to the King's Exchequer; ye shall not look for gifts or other cause, but well and truly ye shall do your office as Justice of the Peace in that behalf; and that ye take nothing for your office of Justice of the Peace to be done but of the King's fees accustomed and cost limited by the Statutes; and ye shall not direct or cause to be directed any warrant by you to the parties but ye shall direct them to the Bailiffs of the said county of Salop or other of the King's Officers or

Ministers or other indifferent persons to do exactly thereof, so God you help and by the contents of this book.

Magistrates heard all kinds of cases, ranging from trivial offences to charges of murder or rape (such cases would not however be dealt with by the magistrates, but would be respited until the next Assizes and put before a senior judge and a jury). However, the Shropshire Quarter Sessions of January 1830 were witness to one of the more unusual crimes to be heard before the magistrates: namely the theft of the hair from thirty-two cows' tails from Mr Thomas Lloyd of Osbaston and Mrs Hannah Hopkins of Woolston.

The *Salopian Journal* of 13 January 1830 reported that John Mate, alias John Myatt, was indicted on two counts of cutting all the hair off numerous cows' tails. The use of an alias may have been indicative that he was no stranger to the inside of a court, but unfortunately records do not survive to confirm this (later Calendars of Prisoners – an official court document produced after each Assize or Quarter Session – record the number of known previous convictions for each defendant, but these only survive

Osbaston, Shropshire. The Author

from the later Victorian period). John Mate was first brought before the magistrates to answer a charge of stealing the tail hairs from eighteen cows belonging to Mr Thomas Lloyd of Osbaston. Richard Page, cowman to Mr Lloyd, stated that he had put his master's cows in the cowhouse at 3pm on Friday, 8 January, but when he came to release them at 6am the next morning, he found 'the hair of all their tails cut straight off close to the end of the tail'. The second indictment accused John Mate of carrying out a similar attack on fourteen cows belonging to Mrs Hannah Hopkins of Woolston in the nearby parish of Westfelton on the night of Thursday, 7 January.

Such mutilation of cows' tails may at first seem simply the actions of a cruel and mentally disturbed individual, but in fact John Mate was perfectly sane, and he had carried out his nefarious activities with a healthy profit in mind. Cow's hair, along with many other types of animal hair, including rabbit fur and beaver pelts, was used in the manufacture of felting for various types of hat.

The wearing of hats was *de rigueur* throughout the nineteenth century, with the perceived social status of people often being directly related to their sartorial appearance. Even criminals often made an attempt to appear properly attired; William Howe, who murdered a gentleman farmer, Benjamin Robins, near Kinver in Staffordshire in 1812, was described in the handbill offering a £100 reward for his arrest as appearing 'clean and rather well dressed, with a good hat, a fawn waistcoat and a long dark-coloured coat', and because he was known for his sartorial

Fashionable hats, 1816. Author's collection

elegance, he was nicknamed 'Dandy Howe'. Consequently there was a large demand for hats of all shapes, sizes and quality, ranging from expensive fur hats to cheaper felt hats made from animal hair.

In the evidence heard at his trial, it emerged that Mate had sold his ill-gotten gains, which amounted to ten pounds weight of hair, to a local hatter, Mr Edward Roberts of Oswestry. He had apparently received a total of five shillings and fourpence in return – what Mr Roberts was quick to point out to the court should be considered 'a fair price'.

The hair from the unfortunate cows could not be produced as evidence, having been mixed with other hair at the hatters, but Constable William Franklin of Oswestry testified that he had apprehended Mate at the house of Ann Edwards, 'a person of notoriously bad character', again suggesting that Mate was no stranger to the criminal confraternity. Constable Franklin, then in his mid-thirties, was the parish constable at Oswestry, and joined the newly created Oswestry Borough force some six years later. The force was established on 12 February 1836 and originally consisted of Chief Officer Jacob Smith and Constable Franklin. It doubled in size to four officers before being subsumed into Shropshire County Police Force in 1861.

There was no countywide police force in Shropshire until 1 April 1840. Prior to that date, each parish had its own amateur and voluntary constable, elected annually (often against his will) and often completely unsuitable for the job. Some constables were elected year after year, and were obviously considered to be efficient, but the majority were regarded in low esteem. Such constables did possess the power of arrest, and magistrates could issue arrest warrants that constables would enforce. Shropshire was one of the first counties to agitate for a countywide police force, with Quarter Sessions magistrates resolving in January 1831:

> that the formation of a Constabulary Force throughout the County [...] with a view to the preservation of the Peace and security of property should be adopted, and that this Court strongly recommends the Magistrates [...] to take immediate steps with a view to its organisation.

This recommendation came to nothing, and in 1838, the Shropshire

Quarter Sessions sent a petition to Parliament in January 1838, which stated that:

> the Rural Police is at present totally inefficient for the prevention of crime, and [...] the detection of it, as the former most important duty is not even attempted, and the latter is performed by office Constables attached to each Petty Sessions. The passing of an Act to enable the Court of Quarter Sessions to appoint and pay out of the County Rate

1752 Arrest Warrant issued to amateur parish constables by a county magistrate. (© Shropshire Archives)

a body of Constables subject to the authority of the Magistrates but placed under the superintendence of a Chief Officer responsible to them for the arrangements and disposition of the force within the Shire would confer a most important benefit on Rural Districts in as much as such an Establishment would effectively provide for the prevention as well as the detection of Offences; for the security of Person and property and for the preservation of the Public Peace.

Shropshire subsequently became one of the first counties to adopt the County Police Act of 1839, which enabled counties to create police forces along the lines of the petition. It was not until 1856 with the Counties and Boroughs Police Act that all counties and boroughs in England and Wales were required by statute law to have a professional police force.

Returning to Mate's appearance before the Quarter Sessions magistrates, as no evidence was produced he may have been fortunate enough to escape the clutches of justice, but instead of keeping his mouth firmly shut and relying on the fact that there was only circumstantial evidence against him, he seems to have been overcome by a foolish desire to create an over-elaborate alibi.

The *Salopian Journal* reported that 'there was nothing to bring home the felony to the prisoner until, previous to the case going to the Jury, the prisoner was asked in the customary form, whether he wished to say anything for himself'. Mate mistakenly took advantage of the opportunity, and in the words of the newspaper:

fortunately for the ends of justice, chose to enter upon a history of his travels on the night of the 7th, and of his adventures during the course of that night and early the next morning; in doing this he, as many rogues have done before, "let the cat out of the bag", for he gave such an account of his buying the hair from a stranger [...] as left no doubt of his guilt.

The process of making felt hats was a dangerous business. Until the middle of the nineteenth century animal pelts were rinsed in a process called 'carroting' (so named because the mercuric nitrate which separated the fur from the skin and matted the fur together was suspended in an orange-coloured solution). Whether or not Mate had spent too much time in Edward Roberts' hat manufactory,

An itinerant hat-seller from the late nineteenth century with an unusual but effective way of displaying his wares. Author's collection

inhaling the poisonous and mind-altering mercury fumes that were used in the hatting process (and which drove many hatters insane, leading to the phrase 'as mad as a hatter'), is open to question, but as a consequence of his eloquent but misguided attempt to impress the jury with his 'honesty', Mate was immediately convicted and sentenced to three months' hard labour, which was to be preceded by a public whipping.

Chapter 8

'From Shrewsbury to Sydney and back again – and back again?' Burglary in Shrewsbury 1832

This chapter highlights a fairly unusual circumstance – that of a repentant criminal voluntarily offering himself up to justice – which in return seems to have treated him somewhat harshly. It also shows the extremely difficult conditions that transported convicts faced both on the voyage to Australia and whilst confined there.

On 27 November 1845 Sir John Pirie, former Mayor of London and shipping magnate, presided over the court business in the magistrates' court at the Mansion House, London. At the end of the routine business a case was presented before him that was completely out of the ordinary.

Mansion House, City of London, constructed 1753. Author's collection

A thirty-year-old mariner named John Potter put himself before the bar as a voluntary prisoner. This was unusual enough in itself, but his story proved to be even more remarkable. James Bradley, one of the principal officers of the court, stated that Potter had recently handed himself over to Bradley as an escaped convict. Bradley had checked Potter's story out and found it to be correct in every respect.

Some thirteen years earlier, on 10 August 1832, John Potter had been brought before Shrewsbury Assizes charged with forcibly breaking and entering the property of Mr William Evans on 5 June 1832, from where he stole goods to the value of thirty-two shillings. Despite the relatively low financial value of the goods stolen, housebreaking (along with burglary, which was basically housebreaking at night) was seen as an extremely serious offence, and until 1833 it carried the death penalty. Between 1819 and 1832 some 203 people were executed for this type of crime – at twenty-one percent of the total of executions carried out during the period in question, this was a higher proportion than executions for murder (nineteen percent). John Potter must therefore have been a very worried man when the death sentence was pronounced. Four other individuals at the same Shrewsbury Assizes (Charles Hazlewood, James Price, Thomas Percy and Joseph Roberts) also received the death penalty.

However, perhaps as Potter's case had involved relatively little in the way of stolen goods, the Royal prerogative of mercy was sought in order to commute the sentence to transportation for life. It is not clear whether or not this was on the recommendation of the presiding judge (who since 1823 had the legal power to commute the death sentence on the spot), or whether a subsequent appeal was made by Potter or his lawyer. As it originated in the provinces this appeal would not have been made to King William IV in person, but to the Home Secretary, who by then had the power to grant such requests. Until 1837 in London or Middlesex cases the king and his council did actually sit after each Old Bailey session to determine whether or not the death sentence should stand.

Potter was therefore spared a public hanging, and instead was sent to a convict prison awaiting transportation to Australia.

Transportation to Australia had begun in 1787, but transportation to other parts of the British Empire had taken place for many years before this, including the west coast of Africa, the Caribbean and America. The latter country was a favourite destination to send convicts until the American War of Independence in 1776 had resulted in America refusing to accept any more British convicts. Although seen as a relatively cheap method of punishing offenders in the eighteenth century, just getting the convicts to the convict ship could be an expensive business. The surviving accounts of a Shropshire parish constable, William Davies, from 1774 show just how costly the process could be:

24 April 1774 - A Bill of Expenses to William Davies for Conveying Catherine Jones to Shrewsbury, Salop to be Transported 1774

Paid to Gaoler of Salop for his Trouble & the Convicts Carriage from Salop to Bristol - £2-2s.-0d.

Paid to Ditto for the Merchants to Convey the Convict to America - £5-5s.-0d.

To the Hire of three horses to Salop at 5s. Each - £0-15s-0d

To my Self two Days at 2s.6d. per Day - £0-5s.-0d.

Man two Days at 1s. per Day - £0-2s.-0d.

To Eatables two Days for two - £0-4s.-0d.

To Liquor - £0-3s.-6d.

To Turnpikes - £0-1s.-0d.

To Letters from Bristol on the Convict's account - £0-0s.-8d.

To Horse Hay and Corn - £0-3s.-6d.

Despite such costs, transportation continued until 1868. By the first decades of the nineteenth century some male convicts sentenced to be transported in fact served out much of their sentences on board prison hulks – old decommissioned warships without masts – the men being employed on public works such as road construction. In 1833 it was reported that some 8,000 men were on board such ships in British ports such as Woolwich or Portsmouth. Conditions aboard the hulks were generally acknowledged to be appalling. Potter was therefore again lucky in that he finally boarded convict ship *Mangles* on 8 December 1832, and set sail for New South Wales. The 594-ton ship *Mangles* was one of a fleet of ships owned by E & C F Mangles, a company which by then had secured a lucrative slice of the convict transportation market; the Mangle family also became an important family in Australia. This was the sixth such journey made by *Mangles* and on this occasion was captained by Master Mariner William Warr. Although both the ship and the crew were used to the journey, it was still a highly hazardous one, and both crew and transportees must have breathed a collective sigh of relief when it docked in Sydney, New South Wales, on 19 March 1833 after a three-month voyage halfway across the world. Of the 236 all-male convicts aboard, only one had died during the crossing. The convicts were normally guarded during the long voyage by pensioner guards who were also on their way to a new life with their families in Australia.

Life for transported convicts was very different from what they could expect in an English prison. John Potter was given a convict number (4323) and was allocated to a Mr Templeton of Concord

Richmond Bridge, Tasmania – the first stone bridge in Australia, constructed in 1824 entirely by convict labour. The Author

(an area of Sydney, now a sprawling suburb). A report from the *Van Diemen's Almanac* of August 1832 stated that:

> *All persons who are transported are placed, without reference to any previous circumstances whatever, either in the public service, or are assigned to private individuals immediately upon landing [...]. Those who are assigned to private individuals must be bona fide in the service of their masters. They are not allowed to live away from his roof, must not be paid wages, not work for themselves, can go nowhere without a pass, in fact, although possessing a sort of comparative liberty, are still under the closest control imaginable.*

They were put to work doing anything that was required in order to make the relatively new colony of Australia thrive. Most of the work was of a backbreaking manual nature, as much of Australia remained an untamed wilderness, and life could often be extremely harsh. Many public buildings and edifices were constructed by convicts, including the first stone bridge to be erected in Australia at Richmond, Tasmania.

It was also true however that a transported convict could, through diligence, hard work and a little luck, serve out his or her sentence and then make a new life for him/herself after receiving a certificate of freedom. This was the last stage in a bureaucratic system which aimed to reintegrate convicts into society. After a certain period of time (normally four years for those serving a seven-year sentence, six years for those serving a fourteen-year sentence, and eight years for those serving a life sentence), convicts with a good conduct record could be given a Ticket-of-Leave – basically a form of parole which gave them limited freedom to work for themselves in a restricted geographical area. If they maintained an unsullied record, they could then apply for a Conditional Pardon, which allowed them further rights, and finally, after their sentence had been served, they would be given a coveted Certificate of Freedom, enabling them to receive the same rights and responsibilities as free settlers. This also applied to those serving life sentences – then as now, life very rarely meant life; it was usual for a 'lifer' to serve upwards of a dozen years before being considered for a Conditional Pardon. Some transportees never received such a pardon however, and the last pardons were given in

Entrance to the Separate Prison, Port Arthur. The Author

1906, some thirty-eight years after transportation to Australia had ended, indicating that some unfortunate individuals spent the majority of their adult lives as convicts. Anyone such as Potter who had received a life sentence was not allowed to return to England even after receiving their Certificate of Freedom – they were effectively banished for life, even though they could emigrate from Australia to other countries such as America.

Documents relating to John Potter during his enforced sojourn in New South Wales are scarce, and the situation is further complicated by the fact that another John Potter of similar age was convicted at Gloucester in 1832 and was also transported (in this case for seven years) on the same ship as the subject of this case. However, what is clear is that 'our' John Potter did not relish the thought of remaining in Australia for the rest of his life. He stated in his evidence to Officer Bradley that in Sydney he witnessed first-hand 'the miserably immoral conditions of his fellow-convicts'. At

Port Arthur Convict Establishment – home to a notorious regime for recidivists and hardened transportees. The Author

some stage during his time in Australia he therefore made up his mind to escape. No records survive showing how he accomplished this – and it must have been a difficult task as convicts were monitored regularly. However, at least he did not have the natural elements to face as an additional hazard, unlike those convicts who were later transported to Western Australia between 1850 and 1868. There are several accounts of escaped convicts simply disappearing into the Outback and not being found for months, when their often dismembered corpses were discovered after they had died of thirst or sunstroke, and their bodies had been half-eaten by wild animals. Even if an escape attempt was initially successful, the escapee faced the problem of how to return to his home and family.

Potter was probably successful at his first attempt, as failed escapees or persistent offenders were normally sent to convict establishments such as Port Arthur in Tasmania, where they endured a much harsher regime, including long periods of solitary confinement in a purpose-built Separate Prison, when they had no direct contact with another human being for between four and twelve months, and where the silent warders wore cloths over their feet to prevent any sound reaching the prisoners. This often drove the inmates mad, and Port Arthur was a much-feared and hated destination as a result.

Potter stated that he made his successful escape in December 1839 and managed to gain a position on an American-owned vessel. He arrived in America some months later and then became an employee of the Hudson's Bay Company, being sent to Africa. He then stated that he worked hard for a long period of time, eventually becoming a seaman on the *John Gray*, sailing between Greenock in Scotland and Bombay, India.

During the outward voyage of this journey, Potter claims that he discovered God, and that from this moment on, he felt the need to read his fellow mariners 'a strong lesson upon the nature and effects of their crimes and errors'. Whilst in India, he met with a clergyman in Calcutta and discussed with him the possibility of returning to England and confessing his sins to the authorities.

He applied to Sir John Pirie, who was sympathetic to his cause, to the extent of offering to find him gainful employment, but stated that as a magistrate he had to submit Potter's case to the Secretary of State (Home Secretary). Such an application was made to Sir James Graham, who, whilst similarly sympathetic, felt unable to issue a pardon, and stated that Potter must undergo a further trial concerning his escape from Sydney.

Potter was therefore sent directly to Newgate prison, where he awaited the outcome of the Grand Jury. This body of men found that there was a case for Potter to answer and consequently issued a 'True Bill' which gave permission for the case to be heard at the next sitting of the New Court of the Old Bailey.

The trial took place on 3 February 1846 and Potter, clearly hoping for the mercy of the judge as a repentant sinner, pleaded 'guilty'. After hearing the case the judge, despite being clearly sympathetic to Potter's situation, opined that although 'there was

Handmade convict brick built into one of the walls of Hobart Gaol, Tasmania, with three finger impressions. The Author

no moral guilt in the offence which he [Potter] had committed', there remained a case to answer in law – Potter was, and remained, an escaped convict. The judge further stated that the penalty for this transgression was fixed in law and that therefore Potter was to remain in Newgate for a further three months and was then 'to be transported beyond the seas for the term of his natural life'.

If genuinely repentant, Potter must have been absolutely devastated by this decision; for six years he had successfully escaped the life of a transported convict and lived a blameless and productive existence. It is obviously difficult to discern his motives for handing himself over to the authorities, but his explanation has the ring of truth about it, and it is difficult not to feel some sympathy for him.

An appeal was immediately made to commute the sentence due to the unusual circumstances surrounding Potter's reappearance in England. Perhaps to strengthen his appeal, Potter made it clear that he wanted to return to Sydney as a free man in order to spread the word of God to his former fellow prisoners. On 1 March 1846 he was formally granted a full Royal Pardon from Queen Victoria. If he had been forced to return to Australia as a transportee, his feelings would surely have mirrored those of the unknown individual who left the deep impressions of his fingers in the hand-made convict brick depicted on the previous page; one can imagine his fingers digging into the wet clay as he thought of his lost opportunities.

Chapter 9

'I have been murdered by a villain!' Attempted Murder in Ludlow 1840

This chapter illustrates the consequences of a premeditated murderous attack that went badly wrong, together with the limitations of forensic detection in the early Victorian period. It also shows the self-delusional capability of a devious and dangerous would-be assassin, who despite being caught almost literally red-handed, refused to acknowledge his guilt.

Early on the morning of Thursday, 20 August 1840, a twenty-five-year-old man named Josiah Misters emerged from underneath the bed of room 17 at the Angel Inn, Ludlow, where he had been lying on the dusty floor for a number of hours. He had just one thing on his mind – murder. He quietly stood up, and taking out a cut-throat razor, swiftly moved to the head of the bed, in which his intended victim slept, blissfully unaware of his imminent danger. Misters opened the razor and brought it down across the sleeping man's neck. Fortunately, the occupant of the bed was a light sleeper, and feeling the razor cutting across his throat, immediately screamed and put up a determined struggle, receiving several further cuts to his face and neck. Misters ran out of the room, leaving its occupant bleeding severely from the throat.

Josiah Misters' best-laid plans had therefore come to nothing; he had failed in his objective of robbery and murder. However, it soon became apparent that matters were even worse from Misters' point of view – not only had he fled the scene, leaving his victim still clinging to life, but he had also attacked the wrong man! Earlier in the week, several cattle-dealers and butchers had converged on Ludlow for the important cattle fair which was due to be held on the Thursday. One such visitor was Misters' intended victim, Mr William Ludlow, a butcher and cattle dealer hailing

The Angel Inn, *Ludlow.* The Author

from Birmingham, from where he had travelled on the Red Rover coach, arriving on Wednesday evening. Mr Ludlow was a well-known figure in Ludlow and frequently stayed at the Angel Inn. On the evening of Wednesday, 19 August he had arrived in Ludlow at a little before 9pm. After his arrival at the Angel Inn, Mr Ludlow ordered tea in the 'commercial room' of the hotel, whereupon he met Josiah Misters, whom he recognized from a previous meeting at Shrewsbury cattle-fair held on 12 August. Misters stated that he was the brother of another Mr Misters, a maltster of Birmingham and a friend of Mr Ludlow. Misters also enquired as to the health of a Mr Spiers, an innkeeper in Birmingham who was another friend of Mr Ludlow.

Mr Ludlow retired to his bedroom just after midnight after saying goodnight to his new acquaintance. The bedroom that he had been allocated however was not room 17 in which he usually stayed, as this was currently being occupied by another guest, thirty-year-old Mr William Miller Mackreth, a commercial traveller and accountant from a lead-smelting works in Bristol.

It is not known whether or not Mr Ludlow was a superstitious man, but he certainly must later have thought himself extremely fortunate to have been allocated room 13 rather than his usual room 17, as at around 4am he, along with the other guests in the hotel, was awakened by cries of 'Fire!' As he and the other guests milled about the hotel, they discovered a man lying on

Josiah Misters in the dock.
(© Shropshire Archives, reproduced with permission from www.secretshropshire.org.uk)

the floor at the top of a flight of stairs, bleeding heavily from a cut across his throat. The unfortunate individual turned out to be Mr Mackreth, who was so badly injured that he could not speak, but instead a pen and paper were brought to him, and it was reported that he wrote upon the paper 'I have been murdered by a villain!' A surgeon, Dr Crawford from Shrewsbury, was fortunately also staying at the Angel and he was immediately called for. He sewed up the gaping wound on Mr Mackreth's neck, but the victim of the unprovoked attack remained dangerously ill. A police officer, Richard Hammonds, was also called for, and he conducted a thorough search of the scene of the crime.

During the fracas, it was remarked to Mr Ludlow that his friend was not to be seen. Mr Ludlow stated that he was not aware of any friend of his staying at the hotel, but that he had struck up a conversation with a person, Mr Misters, whom he had met once previously. Several of the guests, together with Officer Hammonds, proceeded to Misters' room, where he was found apparently sleeping with the bedclothes pulled over his head. When he was awakened, he appeared shocked and confused – as well he might, seeing his intended victim, Mr Ludlow, alive and well before him in his own bedroom.

Despite certain doubts being entertained regarding Misters' behaviour, he was allowed to dress and go downstairs with the other awakened guests. He was subsequently seen to go into the yard of the hotel, carrying a bundle under his coat. He returned shortly afterwards and later entered the commercial room with the intention of

William Miller Mackreth. (© Shropshire Archives, reproduced with permission from www.secretshropshire.org.uk)

having his breakfast. However, his actions and overall demeanour had by now aroused considerable suspicion, and he was arrested by another police officer, Constable Davies.

Due to the extremely serious nature of Mr Mackreth's injuries, it was thought prudent for the Ludlow Borough magistrates to attend him in his sickbed in order to hear his account of events. Despite his injuries, Mr Mackreth managed to give a full statement in which he told of his waking up after feeling something at his throat. He managed to push his attacker away and broke a pane of window glass in order to raise the alarm. He was certain that he had locked the bedroom door before retiring to bed and was of the opinion that someone must have been already concealed in his room before he went to sleep. He rather poignantly ended his statement by saying 'I had everything to make me happy, and was going to be married in five weeks.' This may have been in response to a suggestion that he had attempted suicide.

Over the next few weeks the full story of Misters' murderous exploits appeared in both the local and national press – the attempted murder generated a considerable number of press reports. It emerged that Josiah Misters came from a 'respectable family' in Birmingham, but that he had previously appeared at the Hereford Assizes in March of 1840 accused of entering a gentleman's bedroom and stealing £15. He was however acquitted of that crime, and since then had been working as a waiter in several 'gin-palaces' in Birmingham.

It further transpired that Misters had been following Mr Ludlow for a considerable time before their meeting in Ludlow. Misters was fully aware that Mr Ludlow, as a cattle-dealer and butcher, often carried considerable sums of money to fairs such as those held in Shrewsbury and Ludlow. In Shrewsbury Misters was found to have visited the Unicorn Inn, where Mr Ludlow had been visiting a friend, and had made several enquires of the chambermaid as to where Mr Ludlow was sleeping.

The chambermaid remembered telling Misters that Mr Ludlow was dining with his friend Mr Jobson at Mr Jobson's house and that he was probably going to sleep at that house. The next morning Mr Ludlow and Mr Jobson returned to the Unicorn, and

The former Unicorn Inn, *Shrewsbury.* The Author

Misters was seen to be listening intently to their conversation, in which the two men agreed to meet again in Ludlow the following week. It transpired that Misters was subsequently ejected from the Unicorn after failing to pay his bill. It was then alleged that Misters determined to follow Mr Ludlow to Ludlow and arrange to 'accidentally' meet him at the Angel Inn. Unfortunately for Mr Mackreth he had arrived earlier on the Wednesday evening and had been allocated the room that Mr Ludlow normally occupied. As a result, Josiah Misters (who had obviously learned that Mr Ludlow usually stayed in room 17) made his disastrous error of judgement.

Attempted murder was a capital offence until 1861, and despite the fact that Mr Mackreth fortunately began to recover his strength after his ordeal, the attack generated considerable police activity. Much of the evidence against Misters was circumstantial in nature, but solid collaborative detective work by members of Ludlow Borough police, Shrewsbury County constabulary, and the Birmingham police helped convict Misters. Officer Hammonds in particular deserved praise as a conscientious and thorough policeman. He traced drops of blood from Mr Mackreth's room to the door of Misters' bedroom, and also discovered a blood-stained cut-throat razor in the yard of the premises next to the Angel, directly opposite the window of Misters' room. He also found traces of blood on the curtains of the window in Misters' room. On conducting a search of Mr Mackreth's room, the officer discovered:

> Marks of a man's fingers on the floor [under the bed], the left hand in particular, as though a person had lain there, and rested on his belly. Where the right hand was it appeared as if a person had breathed on the floor, which was darkened, as if by heat or perspiration, to the extent or size of a man's body.

Mr Henry Hodges of Ludlow, a surgeon called in by the police, also found traces of blood on Misters' clothing, especially upon the right sleeve of his shirt, which appeared to have been hastily washed. It was suggested in court that because of the position of the wounds upon Mr Mackreth that his attacker was right-handed, as was Misters. A pair of men's stockings, washed but still with traces of alum, was later discovered at the inn; alum was used to remove stains from cloth, especially bloodstains. Misters was found to have a small piece of alum in his pocket when he was searched.

A member of the Ludlow Borough police, John Hewitt, liaised with Birmingham constabulary and a search was made of Misters' lodgings in Canal Street, Birmingham. A shaving portmanteau was found, along with one of a pair of cut-throat razors belonging to the set. Significantly the other was missing and was identified as the razor found in the yard adjoining the Angel Inn. The possession of a pair of black-handled cut-throat razors by Misters was corroborated by a fellow lodger, Joseph Vaughan.

Mr Mackreth's health continued to improve, and in a letter to *The Times* published on 23 September 1840, he praised both his surgeon and the landlord and landlady of the Angel Inn for their help in ensuring his recovery from the brink of death. He also stated (and this was before the trial) that 'I cannot attach the least blame either to the landlord or his servant for any want of caution in admitting Josiah Misters into their house'. Such a letter naming the murder suspect would nowadays be used by the defence lawyer as evidence of prejudice before the trial, but in the 1840s newspapers were free to print whatever they liked with regard to murder suspects. Mr Mackreth, in a subsequent letter to *The Times*, pointed out that the company which he worked for (Christopher, George and Co. of Bristol) had funded all his prosecution costs that were not paid for by the county of Shropshire. This was a generous gesture, as prosecution costs could be considerable; it was not until the Prosecution of Offences Act of 1879 that the office of a Director of Public Prosecutions was created. Until then, the victim of a crime, his friends or family had to bear the majority of prosecution costs.

The evidence against Misters, although largely circumstantial in nature, was considered overwhelming, and after a magistrates' hearing, he was subsequently committed to trial at Shrewsbury Spring Assizes. He appeared before Mr Baron Gurney on Tuesday, 23 March 1841. It emerged from the trial that the attack on whom Misters supposed to be Mr Ludlow had been planned from at least early August 1840. Mr William Wright met the prisoner at the Green Man inn in Coleshill, Birmingham, and Misters asked him when Shrewsbury Fair took place. Mr Wright told him and also informed him that Mr Ludlow normally stayed at the Unicorn when attending the fair.

Mr Mackreth, who by now had recovered enough to give evidence in person, stated that he could not positively identify Misters as his attacker because it was dark, but that he had seen him shortly after the attack, when Misters entered Mr Mackreth's bedroom asking if anyone had seen his stockings, which he had lost. Mr Mackreth noted that Misters' behaviour on this occasion was very suspicious, as he appeared abnormally light-hearted after such a distressing incident.

The circumstantial evidence against Misters continued to mount; a bunch of matches ('lucifers') was produced, having being found under Mr Mackreth's bed, and Mr Mackreth stated that he had no matches in his possession at the time of the attack. However, it could not definitely be proved that these belonged to Misters. His defence argued that the blood stains could have been acquired at any time after the attack, as several people including Misters entered Mr Mackreth's bedroom. In a similar manner, it was argued, ownership of the blood-stained stockings and razor could not be categorically assigned to Misters. Modern forensic science would undoubtedly have established Misters' guilt at an early stage, but in the 1840s the development of such science was still some distance off. In the event, after a trial of some twelve hours, the jury retired for half-an-hour before returning a verdict of 'guilty'. Misters, who continued to protest his innocence, was led away from the dock in tears after the judge pronounced the death sentence.

Rather surprisingly, both the prosecution counsel and the victim of Misters' attack lobbied the Home Secretary for a commutation of the death sentence to one of transportation for life. There was considerable debate as to whether or not a reprieve would be issued – even Charles Dickens referred to Misters' case in a letter to a friend in March 1841. However, no reply was received, and on the morning of Saturday, 3 April 1841 Misters was escorted to the scaffold on the gatehouse of Shrewsbury Gaol. He was hanged shortly before midday, in front of a crowd of hundreds, and continued to protest his innocence until his end. He left a letter written on the previous day stating that 'I am, my readers, an innocent man'. Both his trial and his subsequent hanging generated much public interest, and it was reported that an autograph hunter had offered the not inconsiderable sum of five guineas for a letter in Misters' own handwriting.

Misters' mistaken victim, Mr Mackreth, fortunately made a full recovery from his dreadful injuries, married his fiancée Jane as originally planned in late 1840, and died at the age of fifty-one in 1862.

Chapter 10

'Transportation for a pair of two - shilling shoes - or not?' Theft at Whitchurch 1840

This chapter illustrates the often harsh penalties that were imposed in fairly minor larceny cases. It also shows that until the introduction of civil registration of births, marriages and deaths in 1837, it was occasionally difficult for the authorities to establish the exact age of a person.

On 4 December 1840, Thomas Warburton, a nineteen-year-old domestic servant was examined before three Whitchurch magistrates, Sir Robert Chambre Hill, Reverend John Murray and Mr R D Vaughan. He stated that on the afternoon of the previous day, around 4pm, a woman came to the back of his master's cottage, and then went to the back of the building. He said that 'I had suspicions on account of the dogs barking and missed a pair of my mistress' shoes'. He went on:

I came into town to the police and got one of them and went to the lodging houses and asked around. I found her at the Bull Ring. She was going quickly along the street. I told the policeman she was the woman. He apprehended her and we searched her and found this pair of shoes (here Warburton must have exhibited the recovered shoes to the magistrates) *in a reticule basket she had in her hand. She said that she had not stolen them. My master is from home* [i.e. was away]. *I had seen the shoes not five minutes before she came to the cottage. I have seen her at Captain Way's frequently before begging.*

Mr Warburton was a servant to Captain Holroyd Fitzwilliam Way and his wife Isabella Harriet (née Kenrick). The young couple (Captain Way was thirty-one years old, his wife thirty) lived near

Whitchurch at Alport Cottage. It appears that the suspected woman had been a frequent caller at the door of the cottage and had been seen begging in the vicinity. The next examinee before the magistrates was Constable William Hemming. He was nearly thirty at the time, and is listed in the 1841 census as living in Madeley. He told the magistrates that he and Thomas Warburton had found the suspected woman down Green End, one of the major streets leading to the Bull Ring in the centre of Whitchurch. He acted in the best traditions of the police and 'tapped her on the shoulder', stating that he suspected her of the theft of a pair of shoes from Alport Cottage. He then arrested the woman on suspicion of theft and accompanied her back to Alport Cottage, where Mrs Way identified the shoes found on the suspect's person as belonging to her.

The next person to appear before the magistrates was the suspected woman. Her name was Eleanor Bradshaw, and she strenuously denied the accusation of Mr Warburton and Constable Hemming. She insisted that 'I bought the shoes on the road from a travelling woman, and gave her a shilling for them'. Both Mr Warburton and Constable Hemming were able to sign their examinations with their name, but Eleanor made an 'X' as her mark, suggesting that she could not write (although she may have

The Bull Ring from Green End, Whitchurch. The Author

been able to read).

The above scenario would not have been an unusual one in early Victorian Britain; petty theft was a commonplace occurrence, and such opportunistic pilfering as that practised by Eleanor Bradshaw was one of the most popular ways of illegally obtaining goods or money.

However, what makes the case of Eleanor Bradshaw somewhat unusual is what subsequently happened.

Eleanor was remanded in custody until the next sitting of the Shropshire Quarter Sessions. These took place in the first week in March, and on 3 March 1841 she came before the magistrates, chaired by the Honourable Thomas Kenyon. Kenyon was an extremely influential player in local judicial affairs, holding the position of Chairman of the Shropshire Quarter Sessions from 1830-50.

Eleanor maintained her innocence despite the overwhelming evidence against her. She pleaded 'not guilty' and therefore underwent a trial. Perhaps unsurprisingly, the court did not accept her insistence that she had come by the shoes honestly, and she was then and there convicted of felony: 'namely the theft of one pair of shoes to the value of two shillings'. Significantly, she was indicted for larceny after a previous conviction. This meant that she had been previously convicted for at least one felony (unfortunately the surviving records do not indicate the type or number of her previous misadventures). Although her crime was committed many years before the 1869 Habitual Criminals Act was passed, which made a clear distinction between first-time offenders and recidivists, courts still took notice of any previous convictions recorded against offenders when considering the imposition of sentences.

The sentence imposed by the magistrates on Eleanor following her theft of Mrs Way's shoes (valued at two shillings) was transportation to Australia for a period of seven years.

Eleanor was by no means the first woman in Shropshire to be so sentenced, and she was certainly not destined to be the last. Between 1787, when transportation to the newly colonized Australia began, and 1868, when the last unfortunate individuals were banished from British shores, some 163,000 men, women and children (as young as nine) were separated from their families and subjected to this harsh punishment. Although the vast majority (over eighty per cent) of transportees were male, many thousands of females were also sent to various parts of Australia: first to New South Wales, then to Western Australia, and finally to Van Diemen's Land. Four of the 101 women convicts of the First Fleet were tried at Shropshire Assizes: Mary Bolton (45) was transported for burglary involving sixty-one shillings, Mary Davis (25) for the burglary of twenty-five shillings, Margaret Fownes (45) for assault and robbery of five shillings, and Ann Twyfield (23) for assault and highway robbery (this was probably what would now be described as a street robbery or mugging, rather than a dashing romantic venture involving horses and masks). Shrewsbury had been the scene of the last hanging for robbery in England in August 1836. All were transported on the *Lady Penryhn*, a newly built ship of some 338 tons, which successfully navigated the numerous hazards on the journey, and arrived in Australia some eight months later. Females who were transported faced an even harsher regime than males; they were often sent to 'Female Factories', in which they were subject to many hardships and indignities including sexual predation by the male guards.

Transportation was not only a punishment on those who were forced to leave Britain's shores for an unknown distant land; it also affected those family members who were left behind. In October 1823 Mary Bird was forcibly removed from the parish of Churchstoke in Montgomeryshire to the parish of Pontesbury in Shropshire. Following the Poor Law of 1601 paupers became the responsibility of the parish in which they were born. This was not popular amongst the ratepayers of the parish, as it meant that they had to pay to support a pauper with their own money. The reluctant letter accepting the responsibility of Pontesbury parish for the upkeep of Mary Bird survives and reveals a sorry story of crime and sex:

To the Overseers of the Poor of the Parish of Churchstoke in the county of Montgomery and to each and every one of them.

Upon your complaint made unto us whose names are hereby set, and seals affixed, being two of His Majesty's Justices of the Peace in and for the said county and one of us of the quorum, that Mary Bird, the wife of Thomas Bird, a transported felon, she being now pregnant of a bastard child hath come to inhabit in and is actually chargeable to your said parish, not having gained legal settlement there. We the said Justices, upon the proof made upon oath, and upon due consideration [...] do adjudge the same to be true, and that her lawful settlement is in the parish of Pontesbury in the county of Salop. We do therefore require from some or one of you, to convey her to the said parish of Pontesbury with a copy or duplicate of this order to deliver to the Overseers of the Poor there, to be their procedure for according to the law.

Given under our hand and seals the 16th day of October in the year of our Lord 1823.

M. Lloyd, M. Jones (magistrates)

Mary Bird was the wife of forty-five-year-old Thomas Bird, a labourer of Chirbury (near to Churchstoke), who almost three years earlier had been found guilty, along with William Mason, of stealing 200lbs of hay from John Broome of Church Stretton. On 8 January 1821 Bird and Mason were sentenced at Shropshire Quarter Sessions. Mason received a sentence of three months in the House of Correction (prison), but Bird was sentenced to fourteen years' transportation to Australia. This presumably had a serious effect on Mary Bird's fortunes. Not only had she lost her husband, but she had lost a breadwinner. It is unclear whether or not Thomas and Mary had children before Mary became pregnant by another man, but the 1820s were very hard times for the poor, and Mary must have suffered greatly as a result of her husband's transportation. Whether or not the father of her illegitimate child subsequently supported her or his offspring is unfortunately unknown.

Transportation from the shores of Britain had started in the seventeenth century, and as has been stated previously many early transportees were sent to Britain's American colonies. However, following the loss of the colony after the disastrous War of

The Gatehouse to Shrewbury County Gaol. The Author

Independence, transportation moved to Australia and on 13 May 1787 the 'First Fleet' of transportation ships set sail on the 12,000 mile journey. Many Australians are today proud to state that their ancestors came to Australia as transportees and to be able to claim that one's ancestor was a part of the first such contingent, a 'First Fleeter', holds a certain cachet, similar to that of Americans who are descended from the first settlers who travelled on the *Mayflower*. A popular Australian saying is that 'Australians had their ancestors chosen for them by some of the best judges in the country'! However, at the time it was a truly frightening and horrendous journey, during which many convicts perished.

Little or none of this history would have been known to Eleanor, who at the time of the 1841 census (6 June 1841) was languishing in Shrewsbury County Gaol, awaiting her fate.

At her trial, Eleanor Bradshaw was described as a widow, and it appears that her advancing years also troubled the magistrates. A letter was sent on 23 July 1841 by the Chairman of the Shropshire

A satirical cartoon, Black-eyed Sue and Sweet Poll of Plymouth taking leave of their lovers who are going to Botany Bay *(1792), which nevertheless serves to indicate the problems of partners and families being split up by the sentence of transportation.* Author's collection

Quarter Sessions, Thomas Kenyon, to the Home Secretary (then known as the Secretary of State for the Home Department), Constantine Henry Phipps, the 1st Marquess of Normanby, asking if the sentence of transportation could be respited due to the age of Eleanor Bradshaw, who was said to be seventy.

On 26 July a letter was written back to Mr Kenyon by Samuel March Phillips, the Under-Secretary of State on behalf of the Home Secretary:

> *I am directed by the Marquess of Normanby to acknowledge the receipt of your letter of 23 inst. and to inform you that the age of Eleanor Bradshaw (70) precludes the sentence of transportation to Australia being carried into effect.*

It seems that Eleanor's age saved her from both a perilous and difficult journey and a harsh punishment for her theft of Mrs Way's two-shilling shoes.

However, it may be that Eleanor, as well as being a thief, was not being completely truthful about her age. In the *Calendar of Prisoners* dated 6 April 1841, in which there was published a list of prisoners remaining in custody after their trial at the previous March 1841 Quarter Sessions, her name appears alongside a given age of fifty-three.

In the census of 6 June 1841 her age is given as seventy, but the recording of ages in this particular census was not over-sophisticated; ages were given as the nearest five year age group – i.e. if a person was actually thirty-seven years old, they would be recorded as thirty-five, but if they were actually thirty-eight years old, they would be recorded as forty years old. Therefore Eleanor could have been a few years younger than her entry in the 1841 census suggests.

The taking of the 1841 census remained a tremendous logistical feat despite its many shortcomings; it was the first time that extended and detailed records of almost every person in Britain were gathered and collated, and not surprisingly there was the occasional hiccup in its smooth running. Examples of the difficulties faced by census enumerators over the years can be found in the following newspaper report of the taking of the 1911 census:

> *Most of the enumerators found their work of collecting the papers very difficult. In many cases the papers had not been filled in when they called, and they had to instruct how they should be filled in. In others they had been only partially filled in, and in others again the enumerators had to make liberal corrections. In one street only one of the papers had been filled in rightly. Some of the people were out when the collectors called, and they had to make several journeys over the ground in order to get the papers.*

In the *Calendar of Prisoners* dated 3 January 1842 for the forthcoming March Quarter Sessions, Eleanor is again recorded in the list of prisoners remaining in custody, this time with an age of sixty-one. It was not until 1837 that the birth, marriage or death of an individual had to be officially reported to the State. Although parish registers had been kept by the Church of England since 1538, following an injunction issued by Thomas Cromwell, Lord Chancellor to King Henry VIII, these were by no means infallible, and despite an Act of 1597 introducing penalties for neglect of entering such details there was no further enforceable secular legal requirement to record an individual's birth, marriage or death.

Many people of course were not members of the Church of England, and although different faiths did keep similar records, the accuracy and content of these varied widely. Many more people, although professing a nominal belief in God, were probably at least agnostic in their private views, and consequently may not have bothered registering such details within their local parish.

An attempt to introduce more comprehensive registration had occurred in 1753 when Mr Thomas Potter, MP for St Germans in Cornwall, and a tireless campaigner for such reform, had put forward a bill to ensure compulsory registration of birth, marriage and death by the local parish minister 'whether the parent or person be Church of England or not'. However, this was defeated in the House of Lords, as the bill had also contained provisions for a national census, to which the peers were fundamentally opposed, ostensibly on spurious religious grounds; many people thought that the taking of a census would bring an apocalyptic disaster wrought by God in the manner of the plague following King David's ill-fated attempted census of the Israelites.

Without any definitive proof of her age available to the authorities, it is therefore entirely possible that Eleanor, despite having had the misfortune to be caught red-handed, may also have had the last laugh at the expense of English justice.

Chapter 11

'Death in the Workhouse'
Murder in Bridgnorth
1852

This chapter deals with two extremely serious matters: murder and the treatment of the mentally unstable in the mid-nineteenth century. It illustrates the problems faced by early Victorians when dealing with highly disturbed individuals who operated outside societal norms, and also the often harsh and callous ways in which those who had fallen on difficult times were treated.

In the 1841 census, Henry Lewis Colley is described as a patient in Kingsland Lunatic Asylum, Shrewsbury (on the site of the current Shrewsbury School). His personal details remain sketchy, but he was born on 30 July 1808 and christened on 8 January 1809 at Worfield (suggesting that either he or his mother Jane were ill in the latter part of 1808, as it was then common practice to christen babies shortly after birth to ensure their acceptance into the Christian fold in case they didn't survive the first few months of their life, infant mortality being extremely high). He is listed in the 1841 census as a shoemaker.

Apart from his state of mind, he was also unfortunate in being an inmate of the privately licensed asylum at Kingsland. In 1844 the Lunacy Commission (charged with investigating the state of provision of facilities for the mentally ill) named Kingsland Asylum as one of only three such privately licensed provincial facilities that it considered to be especially poor in its provision of care, with the clothing and bedding being described as 'filthy and inadequate', and where it was noted that severely ill patients were kept confined in dark, damp cells. From 1845 the Lunacy Commission took over responsibility for all those classed as lunatics, regardless of whether or not they were held in an asylum or a workhouse.

At the time the asylum housed a total of ninety patients, with seventy-nine being paupers and the remaining eleven being private patients. The town of Bridgnorth, rather than the county town of Shrewsbury, had the dubious distinction of being home to the first privately licensed lunatic asylum in Shropshire, which was built in 1792 following an Act of 1774 (14 Geo III c49) which allowed the creation of such institutions. Joseph Proud was issued a licence to keep 'any number of lunatics not exceeding ten' in his property, and two justices of the peace and a physician were appointed to visit and inspect the premises, with the physician receiving £2 2s., payable out of the £10 cost of the licence. These ventures must have been considered profitable by those agreeing to undertake them, as £10 was a considerable amount of money in the late-eighteenth century, and one hesitates to think what the conditions were like for many of the recipients of such 'care'.

By the mid-nineteenth century such undertakings were recognized as being unsuitable, and in 1845 a new County Asylum was opened, partially as a result of the Commission's findings, but mainly due to the efforts of the influential Shropshire magistrate, Sir Baldwin Leighton. Sir Baldwin, who eventually became an MP, was a tireless magistrate who, as the *Victoria County History of Shropshire* states, 'applied himself unremittingly to the grind of county business and, eventually to a parliamentary career also'. He had a great influence on the design, location and function of the County Asylum, which was located at Shelton.

The unfortunate Colley disappears from the historical record for a

Sir Baldwin Leighton MP, JP. (© Shropshire Archives)

decade, but on 9 January 1852 he was admitted to Bridgnorth Union Workhouse after having been transferred from the asylum at Shrewsbury. The Union Workhouse at Bridgnorth was then a relatively new building, having been constructed in 1848, and like many such workhouses, it housed both poor and mentally disturbed inmates, as no legal distinction was made under the 1834 Poor Law Amendment Act between paupers and mentally ill inmates.

Poor relief was an extremely contentious issue throughout the Georgian and Victorian period, mainly because of what was perceived as the vast sum of money involved in the maintenance of the poor. Patrick Colquhoun (a zealous magistrate and campaigning reformer with considerable influence) calculated in 1806 that poor relief had cost the nation £400,000 at the beginning of the eighteenth century, rising to over £2 million by the last decade of the same century, and in 1803 the total cost (excluding charitable donations) stood at over £4¹/₂ million. By the second quarter of the nineteenth century there was an increasing

Bedlam lunatic asylum from Hogarth's The Rake's Progress. Author's collection

determination to address the shortcomings of the existing system with regard to the cost of the poor, and successive governments wrestled with the seemingly intractable problem.

In 1834 *An Act for the Amendment and better administration of the Laws relating to the Poor in England and Wales* (better known as the Poor Law Amendment Act) decreed that the workhouse would become a central feature of the reformed Poor Law. It divided England and Wales into unions of parishes, which were responsible for the construction and financing of a workhouse in each Union. Paupers receiving indoor relief were originally divided into seven classes:

1)   Aged or infirm men
2)   Able-bodied men, and youths (male) above thirteen
3)   Boys above seven and under thirteen
4)   Aged or infirm women
5)   Able-bodied women, and girls above sixteen
6)   Girls above seven and under sixteen
7)   Children under seven

They were all to be given accommodation 'in which they shall respectively remain, without communication with any other class' (exceptions were made with elderly/infirm married couples). Mothers of children under seven were 'permitted to have access to them at all reasonable times'. Married able-bodied couples were therefore forcibly separated and the fathers of children of any age could not gain access to their children. The implicit reasoning was to make the workhouse an unpalatable alternative to work, to be entered only as a very last resort. The workhouse occupants were by no means permanent; records show that individuals and families entered and left the workhouse as and when their personal circumstances altered – if a member of a family found enough work to support their family, then the entire family would leave the confines of the workhouse; if not, then various members of a family might be inmates at any given time.

It was therefore not surprising that in the years immediately after the introduction of the Union system, workhouses quickly acquired an unpopular reputation – a stigma was attached to those unfortunates who were forced to apply for in-house relief as a last resort. This stigma was recognized by the Poor Law Commission as early as 1837 – in the *Circular of Instructions for Guardians*, printed in that year, *Instruction No. 40* remarks that 'it has hitherto be found that, even in the worst districts, not more than four or five out of a hundred able-bodied paupers, to whom it is offered, will accept relief in the house'.

It is unclear as to why Colley was transferred from the asylum in Shrewsbury – perhaps he was no longer exhibiting clear signs of insanity (mental illness not always being a permanent condition), or perhaps it was intended purely as a temporary measure. Perhaps it was a financial decision, as it could cost up to four times as much to house a pauper classed as a lunatic in an asylum compared to a workhouse. In any event, his arrival at the Bridgnorth Union Workhouse was to have a devastating impact on the life of another unfortunate inmate.

John Gitton was born in the St Leonard's district of Bridgnorth in 1803 and came from an established Bridgnorth family which had several business interests in the town. His father George Gitton had set up a successful printers and stationers in the early decades of the nineteenth century and upon his death his two sons George Robert and John had inherited the family business. George Robert seems to have been a lively young lad, with a penchant for writing humorous verse – a manuscript written by him, and dated 16 August 1809, which includes poems entitled *Mrs Waddle was a widow*, *Squire Frog's Visit*, and *Epitaph on a Dormouse* has recently been advertised for sale by a rare books seller.

The Gitton brothers seem to have prospered initially in their joint venture; selling books, stationery, and chemist's drugs as well as providing a printing service for the town. However, they seem to have undergone a series of financial crises and by 1851 the business had hit hard times, with George (who, as the elder brother, seems to have been the senior partner) having to sell most of his household goods to pay off various creditors.

There is also a sale book of John Gitton's dated 28 November 1851, along with an inventory of goods in the Nock Deighton collection at Shrewsbury Record Office, which suggests that John also suffered heavily in the downturn of the printers. It appears that there may also have been a family row around this period, as George is listed in the 1851 census as living in the family home in High Street, Bridgnorth, with his wife and family, but John is listed as an inmate in Bridgnorth Union Workhouse. His occupation is given as bookseller/stationer, but it is surprising that his brother seems to have not invited him into the family home and instead was prepared to see him suffering the harsh regime of the workhouse. This was to prove a fatal decision. It was not unusual for people to move in and out of the workhouse during the nineteenth century – their presence in the workhouse was dependent on the 'boom and bust' nature of the economy of the time.

Both Colley and Gitton were inmates at Bridgnorth workhouse for several months, but on the evening of 29 March 1852 they were apparently both in the able-bodied men's dayroom of the building, along with whom the newspapers described as 'a blind idiot boy',

Bridgnorth Union Workhouse, built in 1848, and now providing sheltered accommodation for the elderly. The Author

who unfortunately was not in a fit mental state to give any evidence with regard to subsequent events. There appears to have been no simmering argument between the two other inmates, or any other signs of tension, but at the call to prayers at around 8pm in the boardroom, another inmate, Alfred Oakes, entered the able-bodied men's dayroom in order to collect his coat. He heard groaning and discovered to his horror that John Gitton had been brutally attacked and was lying in agony near the fireplace. Gitton had been struck at least three times on the head, and the resulting horrific injuries, which had split his skull apart and exposed his brain, rendered him both speechless and unconscious. He died shortly after the gruesome discovery of his mutilated body was made, and the murder weapon was also soon recovered. A carpenter's axe, which according to *The Times* was 'covered with human hair, brains and blood', was picked up from an adjoining room.

The alarm was immediately raised, and the workhouse master, Mr Barber, was informed of the tragedy. It was observed that Colley had suddenly got up during the prayer session and left the workhouse precinct. A search was made and he was subsequently found wandering through the town with blood on his trousers. He was arrested, but protested his innocence, stating that the governor of the workhouse had given him permission to leave the workhouse premises.

A coroner's inquest was quickly held in the boardroom of the workhouse concerning the body of Gitton, presided over by Mr W D Matte, with the jury unsurprisingly returning a unanimous verdict of 'Wilful Murder against Henry Lewis Colley'. A warrant dated 1 April 1852 was issued for his detention. He was then remanded in custody at Shrewsbury Gaol to await trial at the next Shropshire Assizes.

His trial took place on 29 July 1852 at Shrewsbury, and he was provided with a defence counsel, Mr Skinner. Colley, described as 'a heavy-faced, quiet looking individual' who could read but not write, was put to the bar and when the charge of 'Wilful Murder' was read to him he immediately pleaded 'guilty'. Neither he nor his counsel provided any reason for his murderous action against Gitton; apparently the two men had worked together on many occasions in the workhouse without previous incident, and they had not been known to quarrel.

It was also stated that the prisoner had appeared to be quite sane during his stay at Bridgnorth Workhouse. However, during his appearance at the Assizes, there was obviously considerable doubt as to the degree of his sanity, and the judge, prosecution and defence counsel, and the jury discussed whether or not he was in a fit state to stand trial. It was soon concluded that he was not, and consequently he was further remanded in custody until such time as he was thought to be in a stable enough condition to so do.

Colley was never subsequently brought to trial over the murderous attack on John Gitton, as he was found on adjournment to be insane, and was instead 'ordered to be kept in custody at Her Majesty's pleasure'. He died within a few years of his renewed detention, passing away in Birmingham in 1855.

John's brother George finally managed to restore the profitability of the family business despite the tragic loss of his brother, and he continued in the printing business until the end of his life in 1885. He also kept a series of private diaries for a number of years in the 1860s. One of these has survived for the year 1866 and was published a few years ago by Shrewsbury Archives. It gives a fascinating insight into the daily life of a small provincial town in the mid-Victorian period, and George Gitton comes across as a decent and likeable individual, who mixed freely with all classes of Bridgnorth society. However, despite being written only a few years after the murder of his brother, no mention is made of the terrible incident on the anniversary of his brother's demise.

This, along with the fact that George's side of his family is never referred to in the diary, whilst his dead wife's relatives are mentioned on a fairly frequent basis, seems to reinforce the theory that he and his brother had fallen out some time prior to John's unfortunate and fateful removal to the Union Workhouse. Neither did George seem to have had any qualms about undertaking printing work for the workhouse where his brother suffered his terrible fate, as several notices issued by Bridgnorth Union Workhouse in the 1860s survive complete with the name and address of George Gitton, printer, clearly visible at the bottom of the page.

Chapter 12

'I have only one hand like him, and I will fight him'
Murder in Shrewsbury
1856

This chapter illustrates perhaps one of the most straightforward of all the foul deeds in this book – murder committed in the heat of the moment by an armed and drunken brawler. It also shows that anti-social behaviour is nothing new – it was just as much of a problem in Victorian England.

On the evening of Wednesday, 29 October 1856, Annie Usher was out 'on the town' in Shrewsbury. She was a young woman of poor repute who was known to many in the town as Annie Laurie. For some time she had been co-habiting with an out-of-work twenty-five-year-old waiter named John Hollis, who was also known under the alias of John Williams. Hollis was born in Ercall, the son of a labourer, and had worked at a variety of jobs, including being a moulder from the age of ten, and a waggoner on a farm in 1851.

Annie was clearly enjoying herself in the Market Hall at 10pm when John Hollis met up with her. She had been dancing with a man named Clewitt, and this immediately enraged Hollis, who was known for his quick temper and violent nature, and who had previously appeared before Shrewsbury magistrates on charges of assault against Annie. Outside the Market Hall he shouted out 'What ------ game is this?' and attempted to strike her. It was noticed that he was carrying a clasp-knife with a large blade, and he was then grabbed by another man named Hopwood, who prevented him from hitting Annie.

The use of knives in fights was often frowned upon and seen as a low resort used by foreigners or 'continentals' by both those observing a fight and those reporting upon one: in 1841 at an inquest into the death of one man by being stabbed, the coroner remarked that 'this was a crime of a character […] serious and un-English'. Similarly, *The Times* in 1875 stated, on reporting the death of a man in a 'formal' fist-fight that:

> *It had been generally regarded with justice as a redeeming point in even the violence of Englishmen that they have maintained the spirit of fair play and have refrained from gratifying their revenge, as in some other countries, by the safe and therefore cowardly use of the knife or dagger.*

The two men in this case had quarrelled, but had 'agreed formally to fight it out' and the fight was 'conducted […] according to the rules of the Prize Ring'.

By this time a considerable (and largely drunken) crowd had gathered around the protagonists, and Annie took the opportunity to strike Hollis three times, whilst another man punched him to the ground. Annie then ran across the Market Square until she was outside the Plough Inn, where she met a young man named Benjamin Bromley, with whom she had a brief conversation. Annie was then advised to go home by Hopwood, who offered to escort her, but she said that she was too scared, on account of what Hollis might do to her when he also returned. In the meantime, Hollis had regained his feet, and, swearing at Annie, took another swing at her. She managed to dodge the blow, but Hollis caught her with a kick. She seems to have been a woman of considerable fortitude, and in return struck him again before running off.

Another man, Frederick Pritchard, now directly challenged Hollis to a fight, but Benjamin Bromley intervened, stating that 'no, I have only one hand, like him, and I will fight him.' It is not clear from the surviving records as to whether either Benjamin Bromley or John Hollis had actually only got one hand each, or whether or not they were otherwise incapacitated through injury. He then proceeded to match the word to the deed and shook his fist in Hollis' face. Hollis retaliated by saying that two against one wasn't fair and struck Bromley in the chest.

Benjamin Bromley immediately fell to the ground and Hollis ran off; it was noticed that he was still holding a knife in the hand with which he had struck Bromley. Despite efforts to revive him,

The former Crow Inn, *Frankwell, Shrewsbury, recently converted into flats.* The Author

Bromley was found to be dead. His body was taken to the Salop County Infirmary, where an examination found that he had been knifed in the chest near his heart with a deep cut.

The police were then notified, and after a search of about half-an-hour, they located Hollis hiding in the yard of the Crow Hotel in Frankwell, just past the Welsh Bridge. His clothes were found to be soaking wet and no weapon was discovered on him. The police therefore surmised that he had forded the river instead of risking being seen crossing the bridge, and that he had thrown the knife in the Severn.

Hollis was swiftly arrested and brought up before the Mayor of Shrewsbury, Mr John Hazeldine, and a full bench of magistrates, and was charged with the murder of Benjamin Bromley. He appeared calm throughout the examination, and said nothing in his defence. He was remanded in custody for three days so that further evidence could be amassed against him.

A coroner's inquest was scheduled for the next day on the body of Mr Bromley, who was described as a labourer and fish-hawker, aged about thirty.

The Salop County Infirmary, where Bromley's body had been brought, was the venue for the inquest, held by Mr H Keate, coroner. The jury subsequently gave a verdict of 'wilful murder' against Hollis, and he was formally committed for trial at the next Assizes.

Hollis did not have long to wait until his appearance before the Assize judges – due to a large number of offences a Winter Assizes was held at Shrewsbury, and on 8 December 1856 he stood trial for murder.

The largely drunken crowd that had congregated in Market Square at the time of Mr Bromley's death could be seen as representative of what the upper- and middle-classes of Victorian Britain viewed as a hardcore of itinerant, idle and often drunken working-class men – what were often referred to as 'the dangerous classes' – the term was first coined in the 1840s. The perceived problem was clearly not restricted to Shrewsbury – an enraged inhabitant of Crewe in Cheshire wrote to the *Crewe Chronicle* in August 1879, stating:

> *The increase of drunkenness has become very noticeable in our town, so much so that it is utterly unsafe for any respectable individual to pass certain public houses about the hour of eleven on Saturday nights. It is pitiable to see poor wretches, maddened by their libations,*

The Esplanade Hotel, *Fremantle, Western Australia, opened in 1896, and built on the site of the original convict settlement. The Author*

endeavouring to complete each other's misery by spoiling each other's faces; then staggering home with the blissful prospects of black eyes, aching heads, and empty pockets to greet them on the Sunday morning. [...] We see such a vast number of men, aye, and women too, in a most beastly state of intoxication. How have they got so very drunk? To satisfy ourselves we have only to visit the different gin palaces of our town, where it is astonishing to see how openly and unreservedly the law must be violated.

Prosecutions against drunkenness (including aggravated drunkenness and drunkenness & disorderliness) peaked in 1881 in England and Wales. There were approximately seventy-five offences per 10,000 people in that year, and the rate stayed fairly high until 1901. They declined only after wartime legislation (reducing opening hours and introducing stricter licensing controls) more than halved the rate to approximately thirty prosecutions per 10,000 people in 1921, and halving again to fifteen prosecutions per 10,000 people by 1931.

Despite the fact that Mr Bromley had been stabbed with a knife held by Hollis, and that the suspect was known to have a history of violence, it was decided that his action against Mr Bromley was not premeditated, and the jury returned a verdict not of murder, but of the lesser charge of manslaughter. Consequently, instead of facing the death penalty, Hollis was sentenced to fourteen years' transportation to Western Australia.

From his convict record, we can learn quite a lot about Hollis' physical appearance. He was 'middling stout', five foot seven and three-quarter inches tall (slightly above average height for the period), was semi-literate, had a cut on his upper lip, and had grey eyes with dark brown hair. His occupation at the time of his arrest was described as 'servant'. Although sentenced in late 1856, it was not until 3 March 1858 that Hollis began his involuntary journey to the antipodes. He was one of 268 male convicts who were confined on the *Lord Raglan*, a 756-ton convict ship, constructed in 1854.

Hollis' journey lasted some five months, and the *Lord Raglan* arrived at the newly constructed Convict Establishment at Fremantle, Western Australia, on 1 August 1858. Fremantle was a

Gatehouse and Clock Tower, Fremantle Convict Establishment, built 1856. The Author

small port town just to the south of the Swan River Colony (now known as Perth), and was the landing place for the first arrival of transported convicts to Western Australia. The first such convicts arrived on the HMS *Scindian* convict ship on 1 June 1850, and their arrival caused much confusion in the new settlement, as the convict ship arrived before the ship carrying news of its despatch. A warehouse owned by the harbourmaster, Captain Daniel Scott, was hastily leased by the authorities to house the convicts. Somewhat ironically, this site later became the Esplanade Hotel, one of the most luxurious hotels in Western Australia.

Work on the Convict Establishment had begun in 1851, and it was constructed entirely by convict labour, being completed in 1859. The site, situated on a ridge above the town, was, in the words of Captain Edmund Henderson (responsible for the housing of the convicts):

'in every way well suited for the purpose; it is a healthy and elevated spot – removed from the business part of the town, and within convenient distance of the harbour; in the improvement of which there

will be the employment for the Prisoners for many years after the Government works are complete.

The site proved successful – the prison remained in use for over 130 years until 1991, and is now a heritage site, with a museum and regular tours. It also has an excellent website (www.fremantleprison.com.au) with search facilities enabling one to find out details of every single transported convict that passed through its portals.

During his sentence, John Hollis seems to have managed to kerb his temper as he kept out of serious trouble and was duly awarded his ticket-of-leave at Albany (the oldest European settlement in Western Australia, founded in 1826, and situated on the southern coast) on 27 July 1860. He moved temporarily to New South Wales on 5 October 1863 (probably in search of work), but later returned to Western Australia, dying in October 1880.

Chapter 13

'A clever and successful enterprise' Imposture in Shrewsbury 1864

This chapter is in a somewhat lighter vein than the majority of the others described in this book. It serves to illustrate that an enterprising 'con-man' could go far with a measure of confidence, swagger and an air of plausibility. It also highlights a debate about the amateur nature of the magistracy that continues to this day.

On the evening of Tuesday, 27 December 1864 Police Constable Ward Cross of Shrewsbury Borough Police Force was somewhat surprised to be approached by a young man in the Market Square, who asked for directions to the police office.

Constable Cross asked why the stranger needed the police office and the young man replied that he was in fact a police officer from Carmarthen Borough Police and that he was trailing a suspected thief named George Thompson, who it was thought had stolen a gold watch valued at £50 from a landlady in Carmarthen. Constable Cross immediately took the opportunity to help a fellow officer of the law and took him to the police station, where the young man, who gave his name as John Morgan, briefly showed him the arrest warrant. Constable Cross then secured lodgings for Constable Morgan at the Sun Inn and arranged to meet with him the next morning.

At 9am Constable Morgan duly presented himself at the police station and Constable Adams was detailed by Inspector Davies to accompany Constable Morgan and help him in the apprehension of the suspect. Constable Morgan produced a description of the suspect – 'about 44 years of age, about 5 feet 8 inches high, light

Market Hall, Market Square, Shrewsbury. The Author

hair, a good-looking man, with a light or false moustache'. The two officers searched high and low throughout many of the hotels and inns of Shrewsbury, including the Lion, the Crown and finally the Raven Hotel in Castle Street. The suspect was located in the coffee room of the inn, and was charged with being George Thompson and suspected of stealing a gold watch and a gold ring at Carmarthen. The suspect strongly protested his innocence, stating that he was a Mr Charles Ashworth from Fairfield Hall in Lancashire, the son of a magistrate and was on the way to visit a friend at Stanley Hall near Bridgnorth. Despite these strenuous protestations, he was accompanied to his room in the inn, where Constable Morgan produced a key to the suspect's luggage and unlocked it. The suspect was advised to surrender all his possessions in order to avoid being searched, and Mr Ashworth duly produced £8 17s. 6¼d., a gold watch and guard (not the watch suspected to have been stolen, as this was thought to have been pawned in Aberdare), together with a gold ring. Constable Morgan took possession of these and the prisoner was then escorted to the police office.

At 11am the prisoner appeared before the Shrewsbury Borough Magistrates, where he was charged under the name of George

Thompson with stealing the aforementioned items. Constable Morgan asked for the prisoner to be remanded and to not be allowed to telegraph or otherwise contact anyone, as he (Morgan) believed that an accomplice was still at large. Mr Ashworth (aka George Thompson) was then taken into custody in the police superintendent's house, whilst Constable Morgan, accompanied by Constable Adams, went to Shrewsbury railway station, where Constable Morgan wrote and posted a letter to his Superintendent, telling him of the successful capture of George Thompson, and informing him that he was going to Aberdare in order to fetch the watchmaker who had bought the stolen watch from Thompson. Constable Morgan then boarded the train, no doubt with the hearty congratulations of Constable Adams of a job well done ringing in his ears.

This praise would indeed have been well deserved – a dogged and determined officer of the law chasing after a known thief, and apprehending him with commendable zeal; not only that, but highlighting the value of cooperation between different police forces – except for one small fact.

That small fact was that not a word of it was true – Shrewsbury Borough Police, along with Shrewsbury Borough magistrates, not to mention Mr Charles Ashworth (for that was indeed his real name) – had been thoroughly duped by an extremely ingenious and inventive confidence trickster called Thomas Ellis, who was by now on the way to his home in Liverpool with a gold watch and chain, gold ring, and almost £10 in his pocket!

Shrewsbury officials were undoubtedly completely wrong-footed by this audacious scoundrel, and were it not for the competence of their counterparts in Liverpool, Thomas Ellis alias John Morgan may well have got clean away. However, Ellis proved to be too ambitious and pushed his luck once too often – shortly after his successful confidence trick in Shrewsbury he was arrested at Old Swan (a settlement near Liverpool), where he had attempted to play the same trick with a cattle dealer. It was further discovered that he pawned Mr Ashworth's watch at a Liverpool shop.

If the deeply embarrassed Shrewsbury magistracy and constabulary thought that this was the end of the matter however,

The impressive Victorian façade of Shrewsbury Railway Station built in 1848, from where 'Constable' Morgan made his escape. The Author

they were naïvely mistaken. Brickbats of derision and unflattering comments were quickly sent to them from all directions, fuelled by the press which unerringly sensed that a good story was there to be told. Ellis quickly gained infamy as the 'Shrewsbury Swindler' or the 'Sham Detective' and the story ran for several weeks in both local and national newspapers.

Ellis was brought back to Shrewsbury in early January to face charges of imposture and obtaining goods and money by false pretences. He proved to be brazenly proud of his achievement in pulling the wool over the eyes of Shrewsbury's police and magistrates, showing his pleasure at his carrying out 'a clever and successful exercise'. At the pre-trial hearing before Shrewsbury magistrates he immediately pleaded 'guilty' to stealing Mr Ashworth's money. It transpired that earlier on the very day that he had arrived in Shrewsbury he had been released from Swansea gaol after serving a prison term for a similar offence. He stated that:

The warrant was an old warrant of the county of Brecon, which I found among some papers belonging to one of the officers now at Swansea gaol; and if the police and the gentlemen on the bench had read it, they would have found out that it was dated 1851. I have only to add that the police-constables were excessively negligent or they would have detected me at once. I am quite a cripple, and I always thought that a policeman should not labour under any such defect.

The crowd attending the hearing obviously took a similar view; it was reported that when one of the magistrates who had originally entertained Ellis' deception left the courtroom, 'the crowd outside the hall hooted him to such an extent that he was glad to take refuge in a neighbouring building'.

Ellis was formally committed to stand trial at the next Shropshire Assizes. The heated debate about the lack of professionalism of both the police and the Borough magistrates showed no sign of abating in the intervening period however. On 24 January 1865 the beleaguered Acting Magistrates' Clerk felt the need to write a defensive letter to *The Times*, setting out the reasons for the apparent lack of care taken by the magistrates and himself during the events of the previous month. He stated that 'as the evident aim and object of the greater portions of the articles [which had appeared in both provincial and national papers] is to hold up and expose to ridicule and contempt the magisterial Bench of this Borough' he wanted to put the record straight. He claimed that the warrant produced by Ellis ' bore every appearance of being a genuine document even to a practised eye, and was perfectly regular in every respect, except that it had not been endorsed [...] by a Shrewsbury magistrate'. He further claimed that this was perfectly normal, and that a police officer could legally apprehend a person charged with felony without a warrant [whilst this was technically correct it was frowned upon as it left the officer open to a legal action in the event of a false arrest].

The Acting Magistrates' Clerk also thought it necessary to state that Ellis was believed to be the son of a former police inspector, and as such would have been familiar with the behaviour of police officers (it was later reported that he was the son of an Everton butcher). He also drew attention to what he called the 'extraordinary demeanour' of Mr Ashworth, whom he claimed made no attempt to clear his name at the time of his appearance before the Shrewsbury magistrates. Finally he defended the magistrates' decision to accede to Ellis' wish that Mr Ashworth not be allowed to make contact with anyone else after his arrest, claiming that this was 'dictated merely by excess of caution'.

The letter appears to have cut little ice with some of the disgruntled residents of Shrewsbury however; some three days later another letter appeared, written by 'A Shrewsbury Burgess', in which the writer completely dismissed the Acting Magistrates' Clerk's defence, calling the affair 'a bungle from beginning to end'. He raised the question of who was going to pay for the unfortunate debacle, stating that 'Borough funds are threatened with the entire expense of this prosecution', but made it clear that as a councillor he would endeavour to ensure that the magistrates footed the bill from their own pockets. Finally, he made it clear to readers that he supported the introduction of stipendiary (paid) magistrates in order to ensure that the amateurish mistakes made by the Shrewsbury magistrates would not be repeated elsewhere in the future.

This latter debate is still raging in the English legal system. There are currently some 30,000 lay (unpaid) magistrates in England, who deal with over ninety-seven per cent of all criminal cases brought before English courts. It has been estimated that to replace them with professional stipendiary magistrates (otherwise known as District Judges) would cost in excess of £100 million. Although unpaid and therefore amateur, lay magistrates do now receive a considerable amount of training for their post, and always have the services of a trained legal Clerk of the Court to turn to in respect of legal matters. There are currently around 100 District Judges in England, with half of them sitting in London and the rest in large towns and cities, and their starting salary is around £96,000 per year.

Returning to Thomas Ellis' escapade, Mr Charles Ashworth also felt compelled to reply to the Acting Magistrates' Clerk's letter. He referred to this missive as a total misrepresentation of the facts, and that he was given no opportunity by the Shrewsbury magistrates to give a defence. He referred to the loss of his property as 'the grossest swindle ever committed in our days', and also lamented the fact that not one of the Shrewsbury magistrates had offered either an apology or compensation for his losses.

Ellis was brought before Justice Keating at the Shrewsbury Assizes on Friday, 24 March 1865 and was defended by a barrister, Mr Neale. The case generated huge excitement in Shrewsbury, with entrepreneurial street vendors offering portraits of Thomas Ellis alias John Morgan for the bargain price of 6d. each. He was treated almost as a returning hero with crowds assembling outside the court to catch the merest glimpse of him as he was escorted in a closed carriage to and from the court. The judge and jury heard the aforementioned evidence, and even the prosecution barrister admitted that the fraud was extremely clever in its nature and that the prisoner's story was a very plausible one.

Police Officer Cross stated that it was a usual procedure for an arresting officer to take possession of any goods or money found on a suspect and pay any expense he may incur out of such money, afterwards refunding the amount if it was proven not to be ill-gotten gains. It transpired that Ellis had first entered the Raven Hotel alone, and come out after a few minutes to fetch Officer Cross – this presumably explained how Ellis managed to get hold of the key that opened Mr Ashworth's luggage. Mr Ashworth also revealed that the prisoner had subsequently written a letter to him, begging him not to proceed with the prosecution and that all stolen property would be returned to him.

The defence barrister, Mr Neale, made the most of his limited opportunity to clear his client's name by ridiculing the magistrates and police, stating that the whole affair was an elaborate hoax perpetrated by Ellis on behalf of some of Mr Ashworth's friends in order to retrieve a gold ring given to Mr Ashworth by a 'fair lady', and that all property would be restored. This rather lame attempt at an excuse cut no ice with the judge, who warned the jury 'not to be added to the list of those who had been deluded by the prisoner'.

At the end of the trial it was clear that this had not occurred, as the jury immediately found Thomas Ellis 'guilty' of theft by false pretences, and as a previous conviction for a similar offence had been proven, the sentence passed by the judge was that he should go to gaol for seven years – this term of imprisonment had only recently been made mandatory as a result of the 1864 Penal Servitude Act.

Ellis was therefore removed from the court and eventually served out his sentence at Parkhurst Prison on the Isle of Wight. He was an inmate there when a major report on prisons was researched in 1865 and published in the following year. In the *Report of Directors of Convict Prisons*, the prison inspectors stated that:

> The general state of the prisons is, we think, now satisfactory; the convicts are certainly worked hard, and the dietary is no more than the most rigid medical investigation justifies us in granting. Every infraction of discipline, especially of violence to officers, and trafficking, which at one time was very rife, has been promptly punished; and on the other hand, the tendency of all the regulations is to encourage the convicts to industry and good conduct. We do not think it wrong to refer to the testimony borne by the Inspector General of French Prisons to the existing convict system in England, in every detail of which he has shown the greatest interest. He says, in a report recently published:

> 'Thus the organization of all parts of the penal system is complete in England; she has model penal prisons; she has intermediate prisons or refuges; she has progressive classification corresponding to the moral condition of the prisoners; she has conditional liberation revocable in accordance with the Penal Servitude Acts; she has also transportation as a half recompense or judicial necessity; she has a special prison for juvenile offenders, and private or public establishments which serve as auxiliaries to the correctional education of this class; she has a special prison for invalid and infirm prisoners; finally she has an asylum exclusively for insane prisoners. All these details form a complete whole of practical punishment and its auxiliaries. Other countries would therefore do well to imitate the intelligent organization of the penal institutions of Great Britain.'

It is unfortunately not recorded for posterity what Thomas Ellis thought of this report, but it is pretty certain that he would not

Parkhurst Prison, Isle of Wight, home to Thomas Ellis from 1865 to 1872. Author's collection

have had such a favourable review of Parkhurst from the inside. Neither do we know if the regulations did in fact encourage him to 'industry and good conduct'.

Chapter 14

'How could anyone so vile engage?' Murder in Longden 1867

This chapter deals with a notorious case from mid-Victorian England that shocked both locals and the wider public. The case is also notable for the offender being the last man to be publicly hanged at Shrewsbury Gaol.

On the morning of Sunday, 22 December 1867 nine-year-old Catherine Lewis left her parents' house at Longden Common, some 5 miles south-west of Shrewsbury, in order to visit Mrs Anne Davies who had a baby that Catherine occasionally helped look after. She stayed with Mrs Davies in her house at Longden village until around 6pm, when she attended the service at Longden Chapel. After the service, she left the chapel and walked to the crossroads at Longden turnpike with Jane Richards, a domestic servant to Mr John Whitfield of Longden Wood Farm,

and John (Jack) Mapp, an agricultural labourer whose parents lived in the area and who also worked for Mr Whitfield. This was to prove the last time that she would be seen alive.

The next morning, her father, Edward Lewis did not worry unduly that his daughter had not returned home the previous evening, as she often spent the night at Mrs Davies'. Between

Contemporary illustration of Catherine Lewis.
(© Shropshire Archives)

9am and 10am John Aston, a waggoner, was ploughing a field near Long Lane (between Longden and Longden Common) whilst John Mapp was spreading manure. Whilst Aston was looking for a whip-stick in the hedge at the edge of the field he came across a child's straw hat, covered in blood, and which had been thrown into a holly bush. Aston showed the hat to John Mapp and asked him to look over the other side of the hedge to see if anyone was lying in the ditch at the roadside. Mapp refused to do this and told Aston to bury the hat. In return, John Aston declined to do this and threw the hat down. Mapp then stated that he would have the riband off the brim of the hat. Aston rebuked him, saying 'you nasty fellow; put it down'. Later that day, Aston picked up the hat and took it to show a fellow farmhand. Whilst he had temporarily placed the hat on a gatepost, local resident Mary Hartshorne was walking past and noticed it. She immediately recognized the hat as belonging to the little girl that she had seen in the chapel the previous evening.

Mary took the hat to Catherine Lewis's mother at around 2pm – by then Mr and Mrs Lewis must have been getting worried as to the whereabouts of their daughter – and when she showed it to Catherine's mother, Mrs Lewis fainted. Mr Lewis was informed and he ran to Mrs Davies' house, where he was told that Catherine had not stayed there the previous night. Mr Lewis then ran into the field where Aston and Mapp were still working, and asked Mapp if he had seen his daughter, as he had been seen leaving the chapel with her. Mapp replied that he and Jane Richards had walked a way with Catherine, before Jane left to go to her employer and he had returned home to his father's house, where he lived. He said that he assumed that Catherine had walked home.

Mr Lewis began a frantic search of the surrounding fields and ditches, and as he looked into a small hovel at the edge of one of the fields, he discovered the body of his daughter on the floor. She was lying prostrate on her back, clearly dead. Mr Lewis ran out of the hovel screaming and ran to get the local constable, Edward Jones. The two men returned to the hovel and Catherine was found to have had her throat cut and her shawl stuffed into her mouth and wrapped tightly around her neck. She was otherwise clothed as normal, but her clothes were all covered with mud, and a brooch

Crossroads at Longden Turnpike, the point where Catherine was last seen alive. The Author

given to her by her mother was missing. Constable Jones informed his superior officer, Superintendent Caswell, of the discovery of the body and at first light on Christmas Eve morning a thorough search was made of the murder location and many villagers were questioned, including the last two people known to have seen Catherine alive: John Mapp and Jane Richards.

Suspicion fell on John Mapp at an early stage. At the coroner's inquest, held at the Tankerville Arms in Longden, Jane Richards recounted that she had heard of him telling the police that he had parted from Catherine Lewis in Long Lane at the same time as she (Richards) left to go home. This was patently not true – Richards clearly recalled the clock of the church or chapel strike 8pm as she left Mapp and Lewis walking along the lane together. She later stated that she had challenged Mapp on this on the Monday evening, but he had denied it, stating that 'we parted as soon as you left us. I took to go slowly, and the little girl went on before me'.

Mary Hartshorne also told of Mapp's evident agitation at the discovery of the straw hat. She stated that Mapp had seen her with the hat on the way to give it to Constable Jones and that Mapp said 'Oh, Mary, Mary this has come to send me back again'. He burst into tears and begged Mary not to speak against him. John Aston also stated that after the discovery of the body, he had jokingly said

John Mapp.
(© Shropshire Archives)

to Mapp that 'Jack, it's you that done it'. Mapp heatedly denied this and stated that he had left the little girl talking to Jane Richards, clearly contradicting his statement to her. The coroner, Mr Corbet Davies, further heard evidence from surgeon Mr Harries of Shrewsbury that Catherine had been stabbed repeatedly in the throat and that her shawl had been stuffed in her mouth probably to stop her screaming. The gashes and the blockage to her airway had combined to cause her death. Her face and forehead were scratched and contused, and her clothes were covered with soil, dirt and thorns. He suggested that her body had been dragged a considerable distance whilst face-down. John Mapp's sister-in-law stated that at about 8pm on the Sunday evening she was outside her house at Longden Common and heard a scream and someone shout out 'Oh, Mother!' twice before stopping. The coroner and his jury returned a verdict of 'wilful murder' against John Mapp, and he was consequently held in custody on the warrant of the coroner until the next sitting of the Shrewsbury magistrates. *The Times* reported that the public house where the inquest took place was packed full of people and that 'popular feeling is very strong against the prisoner'.

Mapp's trousers were also found to be stained with what looked like blood, as was his jacket. There were also recently sponged marks on each knee of the trousers, suggesting that Mapp had been

The Tankerville Arms, *scene of the coroner's inquest into Catherine's death.* The Author

kneeling. Superintendent Caswell gave evidence showing that he made quite a detailed forensic sweep of the murder area; he uncovered a large area of blood under one of the manure heaps that the murderer had been spreading and traced the path of the body from where it had been dragged to the hovel where it was eventually found. The police officer concluded by the lack of blood along the trail that the body had originally been left where the attack took place on the Sunday evening, and that Mapp had removed it on the Monday morning. He corroborated his colleague's findings of blood on the coat, waistcoat and trousers of the prisoner. A pocket knife with a two-inch blade that had recently been sharpened and a brooch were also produced as evidence, having both been found at the prisoner's home. There was a great deal of discussion as to whether this forensic evidence should be allowed to be entered in the court record, as much of it was suppositional and also could not be verified. Forensic science was still in its infancy: it had only become possible to definitively identify a mark as a blood stain in 1850, and it was not until 1895 that human blood could be readily identified from animal blood. This had led to several suspected murderers escaping justice from want of evidence in the past – after a murder at Bath in January 1828 the chief suspect, Richard Gillam, was arrested, having been found with blood-stained clothing near the scene of the crime – but he stated that the blood was that of a hare given to him earlier, and the prosecution was unable to prove this one way or the other. Fingerprinting was still some years off, not being perfected until the first decade of the twentieth century, and it was not until shortly before the First World War that it became usual to dust for fingerprints at the scene of a crime.

Some basic forensic evidence had been gathered by intelligent parish constables and accepted in courts during the earlier nineteenth century – at murders in Bitton parish, Gloucestershire (1824), and in Tilhurst parish, Berkshire (1817) successful prosecutions resulted from the forensic examination of footprints. The former case also involved the investigation of trouser marks made by sitting ambushers, whilst the latter involved measuring footprints and stride lengths and comparing heel marks, boots and shoes at the time all being handmade, and therefore individual. The world's first recorded instance of forensic ballistics took place in 1813 following the murder of a prosperous farmer named Mr Benjamin Robins at Dunsley near Kinver, Staffordshire, in late December 1812. The murder weapon was a screw-barrelled flintlock, found secreted with three unfired lead balls in a hayrick a few miles from the scene of the murder. The pistol proved to be the companion piece to one found by the investigating Bow Street Officer Harry Adkins in the suspect's possession, along with a lead mould. Adkins noticed that there was a slight flaw in the lead mould, and successfully matched the three lead balls with both the mould and with the lead ball retrieved from Mr Robins' body, thereby proving that the pistol used by the suspect in the murder and the hidden weapon were part of the same set.

With regard to the forensic evidence in his case, John Mapp stated to the magistrates that the causes of the blood found on his clothes were twofold – his handkerchief had been used to bind a cut on his hand that he had sustained a few weeks ago, whilst his jacket and trousers were marked with the result of a severe nosebleed. He insisted that he bought the brooch (which Catherine's mother had identified as identical to that belonging to Catherine) from a man in Longden on Sunday night, and that he was not carrying his knife on the night in question. His defence was not believed and he was fully committed to trial at the next Shrewsbury Assizes. Mapp had to wait some three months before his trial on 23 March 1868. He appeared before Chief Baron Kelly, one of the most respected of Assize judges, and being unable to afford a lawyer, was provided with a defence barrister at the request of the judge. Mr Harrington, the defence counsel, gave a two-and-a-half hour spirited defence, arguing that there was an absence of motive and that the evidence was purely circumstantial. The *Shrewsbury Chronicle* reported that 'as a specimen of close reasoning, few speeches that have been heard in our Crown Court of late years have equalled it. Every one who heard it must confess that had there been the slightest flaw in the chain of evidence against Mapp, he must have been acquitted'.

However, despite Mr Harrington's best efforts, the jury only retired for eight minutes before finding John Mapp guilty of the murder of Catherine Lewis. The judge placed the black cap on his head and pronounced the death sentence. Perhaps mindful of the terrible crime that he had committed, no appeal for the royal prerogative of mercy was made on behalf of Mapp, who was succinctly described in the *Chronicle* as:

A man of 36 years of age, about 5 feet 6 inches in height, and he stooped slightly. He could scarcely, perhaps, be said to squint; but his eyes had a peculiar look, very much resembling it. If his features bore any particular expression, it certainly was not that of a thinking or of a sociable man, but rather of a person devoid of anything like delicate or refined feelings.

It transpired that Mapp was an ex-offender who had previously been gaoled in 1859 at Shrewsbury Assizes for the violent rape of a sixty-year-old woman in the same locality as the recent murder. It was reported on that occasion that Mapp tied a rope around his victim's neck, pulled out a knife, and threatened 'to do for her' if she did not yield to his request. There had been some discussion of his sanity, but the judge had ruled that he was sane enough to know right from wrong, and sentenced him to ten years' penal servitude. However, he was released in July 1866 on a 'ticket-of-leave'. Such ticket-of-leave men had been the subject of a concerted press campaign after the 'Garotting Panic' of 1862 had seemingly implicated many ticket-of-leave men in several vicious muggings in which the victim was attacked from behind and garrotted or strangled until they lost consciousness and were then robbed. The 'Garotting Panic' was later exposed as an artificial construct, a crude attempt to boost the ratings of several papers, but the fear of such ticket-of-leave men remained. John Mapp's subsequent murder of an innocent nine-year-old girl did little to quell such fears.

The edict of the 1752 Murder Act which stated that a condemned murderer was to be hanged within forty-eight hours of the guilty verdict had been repealed in 1836, and there seems to have been considerable debate about Mapp's fate, as he was not taken to the scaffold until 9 April. During his time awaiting the fulfilment of his sentence, Mapp had apparently confessed, and the local papers carried a full transcript of his confession:

When I parted with Jane Richards at the Short Lane gate, Catherine Lewis and myself walked together for a few yards. I ketched hold of her hand, and she said, 'Do you live by Edward Mason's?' and I said 'Yes'. When I had her by the hand she began to cry, and I believe she shouted out, but I am not quite sure. She ran to the gate and got over it – I suppose she was frightened at me. As she got over it I was close after her, and when I got over it the gate fell, but I did not fall. When I got up to her she was lying under the hedge, and I asked her to let me do something to her [this clearly indicates that there was a sexual motive for the attack – this was not elucidated in either the trial or the contemporary newspaper reports]. *She said she wouldn't let me. She then told me she'd tell her father. She was crying. I said to her, 'Well, if you tell your father I'll cut your throat.' I then pulled out my knife and I cut her throat. She was lying on the ground, and I was kneeling at her left side. I got up and wiped the knife with some grass, and then wiped it on her pinner. I then undid the shawl and put the brooch in my pocket, and then put the shawl in her mouth. I am not, however, quite certain whether I pushed the shawl into her mouth before I cut her throat or afterwards, but I did put it in. I then got up and turned her head round, and pulled her down the field by her right hand. She was not dead when I started with her, but she was quite dead before I got to the bottom of the field. I put her in the building where she was found. I think the mark on her forehead was caused by the heel of my boot touching her as I pulled her down the field. I did not strike her. I was very sorry after I done it.'*

Despite the last sentence of his confession, Mapp does not seem to have suffered much contrition as the result of his murderous action. Rather unusually, Catherine Lewis' father asked for, and was granted an interview with Mapp the day before his execution, but their conversation remains unknown. Mapp was hanged at 8am from a scaffold erected on the right turret of the gatehouse of Shrewsbury Gaol. His death attracted a considerable crowd, as it was widely known that it was to be the last public hanging in Shrewsbury. Penny ballads were hastily composed and printed in order to be for sale at the hanging – these were rushed out by entrepreneurial printers who could confidently expect to make a quick profit from the large crowd. One such penny ballad dealing with the Mapp case survives, and a couple of verses give some idea of the overblown and sensational doggerel of such songs:

The cruel monster was not afraid
To kill a youthful and innocent maid
Little Catherine Lewis, on a Sunday night
Mapp, without a reason, deprived of life

Oh! how could anyone so vile engage,
To kill a child but nine years of age
Her clothes he scattered over ditch and field
For which he finds now his fate is sealed

From 1868 onward, hangings throughout England and Wales were conducted in private within the grounds of gaols. Public hanging, once thought to act as a considerable deterrent to would-be offenders, was by then seen as being counter-productive, with huge crowds treating the horrific spectacle as nothing more than free entertainment. Many people brought their children along to see the sight, as is vividly described in the *Shrewsbury Chronicle*'s account of the scene:

> *Yesterday morning, even before day had dawned, people wended their way into Shrewsbury in considerable numbers, mostly on foot, but many in vehicles, and, by seven o'clock, a large crowd had collected in the open space fronting the gaol, which crowd was augmented, as time went on, until some five or six thousand persons were disposed in the space alluded to, in Howard Street, and other points from which a view of the scaffold could be had. The walls skirting the railway were thronged, and many adventurous men had collected on the tops of buildings near. It was an orderly assemblage, and the police on duty had no occasion in any instance to interfere. There were well-dressed men, with grave, thoughtful faces, there; and many well-dressed women, too, with nothing in their external appearances denoting brutality; children, most of them too young to comprehend in its full extent the tragedy they were about to witness, with some callous young vagabonds, from whose ranks, according to the notions of society, which, however, are wrong in this, as in many other cases, the gallows finds most of its victims; and 'roughs', whose faces it was not pleasant to look upon, and whose coarse jokes were productive of even coarser laughter. Some Dissenting ministers delivered addresses, as is customary with them at such times, and seem to be tolerably well listened to; and there were numerous tract distributors, acting by order of the Religious Tract Society, who were treated with no disrespect. As the hour of eight approached, and the crowd had thickened, there was the hum of many voices, and it was clear that the coming horrible spectacle was the topic which engrossed all thoughts.*

Mapp was hanged by William Calcraft (c.1800-1879), the official hangman from 1829-74 who hanged at least 400 people in his long career, and who had previously found national fame as the hangman of William Palmer, the 'Rugeley Poisoner', in 1856. However, despite Calcraft's considerable experience, Mapp's was not to prove a textbook hanging – although Calcraft later asserted that death was almost immediate, the general consensus was that Mapp continued to live for some ten minutes after being hanged.

Chapter 15

'Mice carrying matches'
Arson and Theft in Onibury
1875

This chapter shows how significant consequences could result from fairly minor criminal behaviour. It also illustrates how easily large houses constructed mainly of wood could be reduced to little more than a smouldering wreck by a servant with a guilty secret to hide.

Ferney Hall, situated immediately south-west of the village of Onibury near Craven Arms, is a Grade II-listed mid-Victorian stately home of some distinction. It is currently being restored by a couple, who have spent several years bringing the dilapidated mansion back to its former glory after it was previously abandoned as a family home in 1952.

One of the lodges to the present-day Ferney Hall, near Onibury. The Author

However, the grand house currently being restored is not the first to occupy the site. It dates from 1878 and replaces a previous house, built in 1858, which in turn replaced a much earlier house. The house built in 1858 fell victim to fire on the night of 10 June 1875. Many great houses of all periods have suffered a similar fate through either accident or carelessness – witness Witley Court, in nearby Worcestershire, one of the grandest of all private houses in England, which was reduced to a burnt-out shell by an accidental fire in 1937. However, the unfortunate demise of the original Ferney Hall was not the result of an accident, but rather arson.

In 1875 Ferney Hall was occupied by Mr William Willoughby George Hurt Sitwell and his wife and family. The Shropshire Sitwell family was well-connected, being a branch of the Sitwells of Renishaw Hall, Derbyshire (later home of the famous literary Sitwells, Edith (1887-1964), Osbert (1892-1969) and Sacheverell (1897-1988). William Hurt Sitwell was a major figure in the county, being Master of the Ludlow Hounds from 1854-63 and a county magistrate. He was also an extremely wealthy individual; when he died in 1909 at the age of eighty-two he left estate (excluding settled property) worth over £53,000.

Such an important and large house required a small army of servants, and the 1871 census reveals that Ferney Hall supported a complement of eleven, including Jane (or Janette) Kingsland, who was then twenty-nine years old. She was Elizabeth Sitwell's personal maid, a position of some authority in the house, being considered much higher in status than a downstairs or kitchen maid (but of lesser authority than the governess). There appears to be some confusion as to where Jane originated; in the 1871 census she gives her nationality as Scottish, stating that she was born in Dundee, but ten years later she is listed as being of Irish origin.

Jane was obviously a well-liked and trusted personal servant; she had joined the household at Ferney Hall in 1868 and was still there in 1875. Unfortunately Mrs Sitwell did not enjoy good health (she died at the age of sixty in 1888) and Jane was held in favourable esteem and a position of considerable trust by her employer. However, this faith proved to be somewhat misplaced. Mrs Sitwell seems to have been a reasonably caring employer; in 1883 an

1885 illustration of a lady's maid. Author's collection

advertisement appeared in *The Times* stating that 'Mrs Hurt Sitwell of Ferney Hall wishes to recommend her laundress, who is leaving for no fault. Apply by letter to Mrs Bengough, The Laundry, Ferney Hall, Craven Arms.' This suggests that Mrs Sitwell was concerned enough with the fate of her erstwhile laundress to sanction such a relatively expensive way of finding her previous employee a new situation.

In early June 1875, Mrs Sitwell informed Jane, who was responsible for looking after her mistress's personal wardrobe, that she and Mr Sitwell were going otter-hunting with a large party at Builth Wells (the so-called 'sport' of otter-hunting not being banned until 1978). She wished Jane to prepare a particular homespun dress for the occasion, being unable to wear the hunt 'uniform' of blue serge as she was in mourning for the death of one of her family members. For some reason Jane objected to her mistress choosing this dress, failing to produce it for her mistress, and she tried in vain to persuade her to wear another black dress. Mrs Sitwell was not to be swayed however, and Jane was left clearly disgruntled. After Mrs Sitwell had retired, Jane then spoke to another servant, Alice Simpson, of a small fire that had occurred in the house in January, thought at the time to have been caused by a stray spark from a spluttering candle, and said, 'Alice, do you know we have had another fire here?' She then took Alice to a small closet in a wing of the house, where there was a smell of burning and signs of a small fire that was now extinguished.

In the days immediately following this strange outburst, Jane became increasingly disturbed, and begged Mrs Sitwell to send for her husband and not to go on the otter-hunting expedition. She also told Mrs Sitwell that 'the house was sure to be burnt down, as it was built under the planet Mars', and that she should take heed of the previous fires. Mrs Sitwell took no notice of Jane's somewhat eccentric behaviour and left the house with her husband on 9 June. Jane was supposed to accompany her mistress, but she complained of a severe headache and was excused from the hunting party. She was seen by some of her fellow servants later that evening during a card party made up of Jane, the housekeeper, the butler and the gardener, and was described in the trial report as being 'not quite herself' at that time.

Some time after midnight, the butler, Mr Hartshorn, retired, having made his usual round of checking that the house was secure. Shortly after midnight, the Sitwell's youngest child, Elinor (then eleven years old), who slept in a room immediately beneath the servants' quarters, heard the sound of a footstep coming down the stairs near her bedroom. She heard a person walk down some fifteen or so steps. She cleverly reasoned that the person must not be a stranger, as her pet dog, although restless, did not bark at the noise. She went to her governess (who slept in an adjoining room) and told her of the noise, and the governess subsequently settled both the little girl and the dog down before returning to her bed.

Just after 3am Mr Hartshorn was awakened by a knocking near his room, and he rose to find that a fire was raging in an upstairs room, close to the closet that had previously suffered a small fire. He immediately rounded up all the occupants of the house and led them to safety. All the occupants with the exception of Jane were in their night attire; she was wearing the same clothes that she had been seen in some hours before, and this occasioned some comment from the other servants. Jane explained this by stating that she had drunk some whisky and soda for her headache and that she had fallen asleep on her bed whilst wearing her daytime apparel. All of the servants, including Jane, made concerted attempts to rescue property from the burning house.

The following day Mr and Mrs Sitwell returned to the remains of their burnt-out home, having being informed of the disastrous fire by telegraph. During a conversation between Mrs Sitwell and Jane it emerged that Jane had not in fact packed the homespun dress that Mrs Sitwell had requested, and Jane stated that she had forgotten to do so, and that it had been a victim of the fire. Jane's behaviour continued to attract suspicion, and on one occasion shortly afterwards she directly asked Mrs Sitwell if she was going to be sacked. Mrs Sitwell said no, but on 3 July Jane voluntarily left her position at Ferney Hall and travelled to London. Although she was informed by the Sitwells that she would obtain no reference until she had cleared her name from suspicion, she wrote to Mrs Sitwell on several occasions from London and did not attempt to conceal her address.

However, suspicion about Jane continued, and in December 1875 she was taken into custody from her lodging in London. Her personal possessions were searched and a quantity of Mrs Sitwell's clothing was found, including the homespun dress that Jane had claimed was burnt by the fire at Ferney Hall. Other articles of clothing belonging to Mrs Sitwell and her son, William, were subsequently found to have been sold by the prisoner to a former colleague in Scotland and to a person named Grover in London. On being arrested, Jane reportedly said to the arresting officer 'I suppose you have come about the fire at Ferney Hall'. When questioned by a police superintendent about the fire, she stated that the small fire in the closet must have been caused by 'mice carrying matches to their holes'.

This was clearly a fairly preposterous suggestion, especially as the 'safety' match was by this time in common production, having been invented in the mid-1840s. This match, unlike the previous portable methods of fire-lighting, relied on a chemical reaction between the match head and a striking surface. Safety matches were in fact considerably more dangerous to those who manufactured them; 'phossy jaw' (a bone cancer which caused the face to turn green then black and finally to exude foul pus) was commonly found amongst the workers (predominantly young women) who earned their living in match-making factories, and was caused by the high levels of phosphorus present in the production process. The public exposure of this terrible suffering eventually resulted in a campaign fronted by the social activist Annie Besant in 1888, culminating in a successful withdrawal of labour by the match-girls of Bryant & May (one of the largest match-making companies in the world), which led to greatly improved conditions of work.

Returning to the fire at Ferney Hall, Jane also later attributed the fire to lightning. Not surprisingly, her extraordinary explanations of how the fires started were not taken seriously by the police, and she was subsequently brought back to Shropshire to stand trial at the Lent Assizes of 1876 on three counts of arson, larceny, and intent to defraud. The trial was intended to prove that Jane had deliberately set a fire at the Hall in order to conceal the fact that the homespun dress that Mrs Sitwell had wanted to wear had in fact been stolen by Jane.

Jane's trial commenced on 27 March at Shrewsbury Assizes and lasted two days. All of the evidence regarding the charge of arson was admitted to be circumstantial in nature and the judge pointed out to the jury that without the discovery of the allegedly stolen goods belonging to Mrs Sitwell, the prisoner would have had no case to answer, and that the Sitwells had been wise not to instigate legal proceedings immediately after the fire.

The jury retired with a model and plans of Ferney Hall in order to consider their verdict, and returned into the court room after an hour and a half. The foreman was asked to announce their verdict and he stated that Jane was 'guilty' of the third count; i.e. of setting fire to the house with intention to defraud. The judge in addressing

Ferney Hall, 1891. (© Shropshire Archives, reproduced from Leach's County Seats)

the prisoner, stated that 'you were no doubt under considerable temptation, in as much as you had robbed your employers, and discovery was staring you in the face'. In attempting to conceal her behaviour however, she had put the lives of everyone at the Hall in considerable danger. The judge proceeded to sentence her to fifteen years' imprisonment.

In the 1881 census, Jane Kingsland is described as a domestic servant, and is a prisoner in Woking District Female Convict Prison (convict prisons were directly run by the State, unlike the county prisons that were administered by the relevant county). Interestingly, she is described as a widower, whereas her marital status in the 1871 census is given as single. A Jane Kingsland of the right age appears in both the 1891 and 1901 census as a widowed domestic servant at Hove, Sussex, and Kennington, London, respectively, and it is likely that this is the same individual as set fire to Ferney Hall in an attempt to cover up her nefarious behaviour. As her surname remains the same in all the censuses, she may have been widowed before becoming a domestic servant; indeed the loss of a husband may have forced her to become a working woman.

Ferney Hall was rebuilt in a suitably grandiose and ornate fashion, memorably though somewhat unfairly described by the architectural historian Nikolaus Pevsner as being in 'an intolerable neo-Jacobean style', and continued to be lived in by a branch of the Sitwell family, Frances Hurt, until 1952.

Chapter 16

'From what was told her, she had believed him to be dead' Bigamy in Minsterley 1929

This chapter is a rather sad affair wherein a highly decorated war-hero became the innocent centre of media attention as the result of a woman who may charitably be described as somewhat naïve. It also highlights the surprisingly common problem of bigamy in the early twentieth century.

John Doogan was born in March 1853 in the village of Aughrim, County Galway, Ireland. By 1880 he had become a private enlisted in 1st King's Dragoon Guards. The regiment (originally founded in 1685 as 2nd Queen's Regiment of Horse and now known as 1st The Queen's Dragoon Guards) was posted to South Africa to take part in what became known as the First Boer War (1880-81). This confrontation had been brought about as a direct result of the British annexation of the Transvaal (founded and occupied by Dutch settlers since the 1830s) in April 1877. This led to an armed struggle by the settlers (known as Boers) to remove the British from what they considered to be their land (the rights of the native African population was not seriously considered by either side at the time). On the morning of 28 January 1881, the British force of some 1,200 men found itself heavily outnumbered by over 3,000 Boers at a ridge straddling the road from Natal province into the Transvaal at a place called Laing's Nek. The Boers were well-armed with rifles and were also well-suited to such warfare. Despite the danger the British engaged with the Boers in what is now known as the Battle of Laing's Nek. The result was predictably dire for the British: almost 200 men were either killed or wounded, with the Boers suffering forty-one casualties.

A Boer farm in the Transvaal, South Africa. Author's collection

Two of the British casualties were Major Brownlow and his batman (servant), John Doogan. Major Brownlow was wounded during a cavalry charge and had his horse shot from beneath him. Private Doogan, who had already been seriously wounded, displayed almost unbelievable courage by riding into the middle of the Boers, urging Major Brownlow to take his horse. During this selfless action, Private Doogan was again badly wounded by a Boer rifle-shot, but survived to rescue Major Brownlow from almost certain death.

For this selfless action, Private John Doogan was awarded the Victoria Cross, Britain's highest commendation for military gallantry. He became the first recipient of the medal in the 1st King's Dragoon's history, and was fêted by the British press, his actions being recounted in both the *London Gazette* and *The Times*. Neither was his action forgotten by Major Brownlow. William Vesey Brownlow survived the First Boer War to continue his military career, and ended up as a Major General. He finally passed away on 15 March 1926, some forty-five years after his life had been saved by John Doogan. He was a wealthy man and left a total of £41,346, willing an annuity of £20 to his former servant John

Private John Doogan's dramatic and courageous rescue of Major William Brownlow.
(reproduced from www.qdg.org.uk by kind permission of 1st The Queen's Dragoon Guards Regimental Museum, Cardiff)

Doogan in recognition of his bravery. As a recipient of the Victoria Cross, John Doogan became a member of an elite group of men: to date only 1,355 Victoria Crosses have been awarded since the institution of the medal on 29 January 1856 (incredibly, three men have won the medal twice, being awarded bars to their first VC). The medal is a simple Maltese cross bearing the Royal Ensign, and is traditionally thought to be made of bronze from Russian cannon captured from Sevastapol during the Crimea War. It bears the inscription "For Valour" and is worn in precedence to any other decoration. The Victoria Cross could be awarded to any serviceman regardless of rank, but pensions were awarded to all non-commissioned recipients; John Doogan was recommended for an increase in his pension of 6d. per day in July 1898.

The medal was normally awarded in person to the recipient by the reigning monarch, but unfortunately in this particular instance there was an administrative error and due to uncertainty

Representation of the VC. The Author

concerning his whereabouts John Doogan didn't receive a letter informing him of the date of the ceremony (which took place in May 1882) until it was too late for him to attend. However, John was present some decades later when, on the evening of Armistice Day 1929, a grand ceremonial dinner was held in the presence of the Prince of Wales in the Royal Gallery of the House of Lords in honour of the surviving recipients of the decoration. Some 320 holders of the VC attended, with John being one of the most senior heroes present; three decorated men of the First Zulu War of 1879 attended, and John was one of only four such survivors from the First Boer War. This was to be the greatest gathering of surviving VC recipients ever assembled.

After receiving his VC, John Doogan seems to have settled down to a more mundane life as a civilian. He married and had a total of ten children by his wife, Mary, the first being born in 1882, suggesting that he had left the Army by this time, probably as a result of his wounds. He became a Post Office mail driver and in 1891 is listed in the census as living in Welshpool with his wife and family. By 1901 he had changed both location and occupation: he is listed in the 1901 census as living at Church Cottage in East Shinfield, Berkshire, with the occupation of butler – his previous service as a batman obviously standing him in good stead for this role. He seems to have maintained his passion for the military life however; at the outbreak of the First World War (by which time he was well into his fifties) he rejoined the army in a non-combative role of Recruiting Sergeant – his First Boer War record and VC doubtless making quite an impression on those whom he recruited. Unfortunately, despite inheriting his bravery, two of his sons were not so lucky during the horrendous conflagration of the First World War: Jack (John) and Dick (Richard) were both killed.

A grandson, William Richard Doogan, also died at the age of 28 on 10 March 1944 at the hands of the Japanese as a prisoner of war whilst building the infamous Burma Railway, and was buried with full military honours at the Chungkai War Cemetery in Thailand. Although John perhaps fortunately did not live to hear of the sad death of his grandson, his later life was marred by both the death of his wife Mary in August 1924 and increasing frailty. He moved back to the Welshpool area, living at Stapley Hill, Minsterley, presumably in order to be near one of his sons, William (father of the above William Richard), who had married Lily Gertrude Bowdler in 1915 at Atcham and who had settled in Pulverbatch, Shrewsbury, Lily's birthplace.

As a result of his advancing years and ill-health, John needed constant looking after, and his doctor advised him to advertise for a live-in housekeeper. Following the interviewing of a number of applicants, a young woman named Martha Maria Roberts was selected and she moved into John's house in order to care for him. This was to prove the start of a worrying and probably somewhat embarrassing episode in John's life. Although she was some thirty-nine years younger than John, a romantic attachment appears to have sprung up between Martha and the war-hero. It is obviously impossible to determine Martha's motives for this liaison – whether the attraction was genuinely mutual, or whether Martha was nothing more than a 'gold-digger' with an eye to the main chance remains unknown. Whatever the reasons, the couple were married at Welshpool Registry Office on 16 September 1929. However, their marriage was to prove short-lived.

On 29 November 1929 Martha Doogan (formerly Roberts, née Griffiths) was committed and bailed by Pontesbury magistrates (she must have been living either in the village or in nearby Minsterley at the time – and must have known the area well as she was born just over the Welsh border in the village of Llangyniew) to stand trial at the next Shrewsbury Assizes on a charge of bigamy. It is not clear as to who 'blew the whistle' on Martha, but she surrendered herself to the Assize court on 20 February 1930 and her trial took place the same day. The newspapers were not slow to pick up on the trial and it was reported that she had in fact already married a David Phillip Roberts on 8 November 1923 at Wrexham. John Doogan was clearly a completely innocent party in this farrago, and gave evidence to Justice Branson that Martha had told him that her husband was dead and that he believed that she thought he was. Mrs Susie Griffiths, a sister-in-law to Martha, stated that there was a rumour in Wrexham that Martha's husband was dead. Martha, although pleading 'guilty' to the charge, further stated that she had only lived with her legal husband for a week or two before parting, and had heard nothing of him since 1927. David Roberts (who was very much still alive) refused to give evidence in the trial apart from confirming that he was still Martha's legal husband.

It is not clear whether or not this was a genuine error of belief on Martha's part, but the Assize judge, Justice Branson, seems to have given her the benefit of the doubt. He found the prisoner 'guilty' as charged, but only ordered her to be bound over in the sum of £10 to come for judgement if called – a very lenient response. She thereby avoided a gaol sentence. Her marriage to John Doogan would also have been annulled as illegal. There seems to have been no attempt by the couple to continue their relationship after this court case, and it is not clear whether or not Martha subsequently sought a divorce from her estranged husband.

Female bigamists, although by no means as prevalent as their male counterparts, were not unknown; just a few months earlier a case was heard at Chatham in Kent in which a certain Margaret Lush was accused of having married four different sailors whilst each was still alive. Such serial bigamy was relatively unusual; many women seem to have become bigamists as a result of the prohibitive divorce laws of England. The Matrimonial Causes Act of 1878 did allow for a judicial separation rather than a full divorce, and many people chose this as a less costly option, although they were not subsequently allowed to marry again. Although the grounds for divorce were finally made equal for both sexes in 1923 (including a limited provision for consensual divorce), it was still an expensive option (especially for women who generally owned or earned less money than men). It was not until the advent of Legal Aid in 1949 that divorce became a feasible option for many women.

By 1930 there were some 400 prosecutions per year for bigamy and this led a correspondent to *The Times* suggesting that the French system of marking the birth certificates of both parties with details of their marriage should be adopted, thereby making it much harder for a bigamist to get away with his or her crime. This did not happen, but it is clear that several judges viewed many bigamy cases as difficult to pass sentence on and often not worthy of their time or expense. An Assize judge, Mr Justice Rowlatt, commented in 1931 (with regard to male bigamy) that:

It may be a trivial thing or a most serious thing. It may be a matter of ignorance and really no harm done in certain circumstances, or it may be a story of one woman being terribly wronged, and being deserted, and another woman being ruined […]. I think in very many cases of this kind it is a great pity that the law cannot just look the other way.

John Doogan eventually moved to Folkestone in Kent, where he lived until his death on 24 January 1940 at the age of eighty-six. He was buried in the beautifully situated and maintained Shorncliffe Military Cemetery just outside Folkestone (which also contains the graves of at least two other Victoria Cross recipients). He left £853 and bequested his military medals (including his Victoria Cross) to

The grave of John Doogan VC, his wife Mary, and two of his sons who were killed in action during the First World War, Shorncliffe Military Cemetery. The Author

the Sergeant's Mess of the King's Dragoon Guards 'so that they may remain in the keeping of my old regiment'. In 1956 the medals were loaned to an exhibition of Victoria Crosses at Marlborough House and were subsequently mislaid, as by the end of the exhibition 1st Dragoon Guards had been posted to Malaya. In 1997 the Colonel of 1st The Queen's Dragoon Guards received a letter from a London bank asking him to pick up two parcels addressed to the regiment that had been deposited in the bank vaults. Upon opening them, they were found to contain John Doogan's Victoria Cross and other personal effects. John's Victoria Cross is now on display in the Regimental Museum at Cardiff.

Conclusion

T he above sixteen cases demonstrate that over a period of some 800 years, foul deeds and suspicious deaths have never been absent from in and around Shrewsbury and Shropshire. Whilst certain crimes such as computer-based identity-theft or credit-card fraud are very much of their time, other misdeeds such as murder and larceny have occurred since the human race first stood upright.

I have tried throughout the book to give a flavour of the numerous crimes that have taken place in and around Shrewsbury and Shropshire and which are recorded in a wide variety of historical sources (now richly augmented by many research tools available on the internet). Researching the crimes has reinforced my awareness of the tremendous steps in both jurisprudence and detection that have been made since the thirteenth century when the first crime in this book was recorded. No longer is the defendant banned from giving evidence on oath; or is (s)he unable to obtain a qualified legal defence counsel for want of funds. Similarly, several of the foul deeds and suspicious deaths detailed in this book would undoubtedly have been solved much more quickly and accurately had they occurred today – the plethora of forensic tests from fingerprinting, blood-sampling and DNA 'fingerprinting' that have been developed throughout the twentieth century up to the present-day would have made the lives of medieval, Georgian, Victorian and Edwardian crime investigators much more straightforward. Methods of punishment thankfully have also changed from the barbaric physical tortures inflicted on many medieval offenders, through a mainly retributive system to a more prison-based reformative and restorative regime.

However, it is equally apparent that whilst judicial and detective methods may have changed over the centuries, the motives for the foul deeds and murders detailed in the book have not. Humans have remained fundamentally unaltered in the eight centuries covered in this publication: greed, jealousy and cruelty are unfortunately very much still part of mankind's nature.

Researching the cases, on many occasions it has been hard not to become involved with the lives of the participants in the unfortunate events detailed. It is fairly straightforward to establish the how, what, where, and when of the facts surrounding each of the cases. It is far more difficult, if not impossible, to detect the why – the implicit motives behind the carrying out of many of the foul deeds described in the book, and what drove the offenders to commit such deeds of sometimes almost unimaginable cruelty.

Some of the cases evince a sense of pity, shock and horror despite the intervening centuries; others occasion a degree of humour and sometimes even a grudging admiration for an audacious rogue who almost 'got away with it'.

I hope that readers have experienced at least some of these feelings during their perusal of this book and that their interest in Britain's fascinating and well-documented criminal justice history has been stimulated. A brief bibliography of suggested further reading is therefore printed below in the hope that others will become as fascinated and intrigued by England's 'Foul Deeds & Suspicious Deaths' as I have been during the writing of this book. Many colleges and universities offer courses on criminal justice history and as a university-based researcher and lecturer, I can recommend them highly as a source of unending interest and fascination.

Further Reading

Crime and Punishment

Barrett, A and C Harrison, *Crime and Punishment in England* (UCL Press, 1999)

Cox, D J, *Crime in Early-Modern Britain* (Criminal History of Britain Series, Greenwood, forthcoming 2009)

Evans, S P, *Executioner: the chronicles of James Berry, Victorian Hangman* (Sutton Publishing, 2005)

Gatrell, V A C, *The Hanging Tree: Execution and the English People 1770-1868* (Oxford University Press, 1996)

Godfrey, B S, D J Cox, and S D Farrall, *Criminal Lives: Family Life, Employment, and Offending* (Clarendon Criminology Series, Oxford University Press, 2007)

Hawkings, D T, *Criminal Ancestors: A Guide to Historical Criminal Records in England and Wales* (Sutton Publishing, 1996)

Hay, D, and F Snyder, (eds.), *Policy and Prosecution in Britain, 1750-1850* (Oxford University Press, 1989)

Justice

Beattie, J M, *Crime and the Courts in England 1660-1800* (OUP, 1986)

Eastwood, D, *Government and Community in the English Provinces 1700-1870* (Macmillan, 1997)

Landau, N, (ed), *Law, Crime and English Society* 1660-1830 (CUP, 2002)

Parker, H M S, and G Jarvis, *Unmasking the Magistrates* (Open University Press, 1989)

Skyrme, Sir T, *History of the Justices of the Peace* (Barry Rose Publishing, 1994)

Policing

Emsley, C, *Crime and Society in England 1750-1900* (Longman, 2004)

Emsley, C, *The English Police: A Political and Social History* (Longman, 1996)

Newburn, T, and P Neyroud (eds.), *Dictionary of Policing* (Willan Publishing, 2008)

Philips, D, and R Storch, *Policing Provincial England 1829-1856: the politics of reform* (Leicester University Press, 1999)

Rawlings, P, *Policing: A short history* (Willan Publishing, 2002)

Local interest

Conan Doyle, A, and J Tracy (ed), *Strange Studies from Life & Other Narratives: The Complete True Crime Writings of Sir Arthur Conan Doyle* (Gaslight Publications, 1988) – contains 'The Bravoes of Market Drayton', originally published in *Chambers Journal*, August 1889

Cox, D J, and B S Godfrey, (eds), *Cinderellas and Packhorses: A history of the Shropshire Magistracy* (Logaston Press, 2005)

Cox, D J, and M Pearson, *Foul Deeds and Suspicious Deaths around the Black Country* (Wharncliffe Books, 2006) – contains an account of the 1822 Halesowen Turnpike Murder, heard at Shrewsbury Assizes

Lethbridge, J, *Murder in the Midlands: Notable Trials of the Nineteenth Century* (Robert Hale, 1989)

Index